"With impeccable research and long-lived experience, Daniel Reinhardt is winsome in his words about policing and peace. No matter where you land on issues of policing, systemic racism, justice, and the way to peace, there is something to learn in *Rethinking the Police*. Part confessional and part plea, Reinhardt's book refuses to demonize any one entity and puts forth a realistic pathway to reform in our communities and world."

Lore Ferguson Wilbert, author of *A Curious Faith* and *Handle with Care*

"Daniel Reinhardt calls people of goodwill to act against police violence, terror, and the inhumane treatment of Black people in America at the hands of the police. He advocates police reforms that focus on internal structures of police organizations, and he highlights the links between systemic racism, police brutality, and the organizational culture of policing with all the frailties of human failure. In the book, the us-versus-them mentality emerges as a component of the police subculture that serves as the normative framework for police-community interactions. Reinhardt argues that the foundation of police violence solutions requires a Christian response rooted in understanding the nature of police culture."

DeLacy Davis, founder of Black Cops Against Police Brutality

"In *Rethinking the Police*, Daniel Reinhardt speaks not as an outsider but as an insider who served as a police officer for twenty-four years, retiring as a lieutenant. With vulnerability, storying, and invaluable research, Reinhardt offers a thoughtful critique addressing attitudes and practices that contribute to a negative police culture within the United States. In this book, the author invites readers to consider a model of policing that reflects Jesus' life and words on leadership. Moreover, as you read, Reinhardt's burden to see police departments and American neighborhoods flourish is evident. Please look at the author's path forward if you want to see both policing and communities thrive."

Jamaal Williams, lead pastor of Sojourn Church Midtown and president of the Harbor Network

"In *Rethinking the Police*, Daniel Reinhardt has given us a learned and helpful introduction to problems in American policing and has offered a compelling vision for possible reforms. This is a book that Christians, law enforcement officers, and anyone else who cares about justice and safety will want to read and take seriously."

Aaron Griffith, assistant professor of history at Whitworth University and author of *God's Law and Order: The Politics of Punishment in Evangelical America*

"Reinhardt speaks with the heart of a Christian leader, the experience of a retired law-enforcement officer, and the wisdom of a scholar. He not only recognizes real problems in police culture but also provides hope for a better way. Readers are not likely to agree with all his conclusions, but his analysis of the problems is compelling and the uniqueness of his solution is challenging."

Timothy Paul Jones, chair of the Department of Apologetics, Ethics, and Philosophy at The Southern Baptist Theological Seminary and coauthor of *In Church as It Is in Heaven: Cultivating a Multiethnic Kingdom Culture*

"*Rethinking the Police* is a rare example of an author who speaks to changing the long-standing, seemingly insurmountable challenges of police legitimacy in our most challenged communities through understanding history and police culture. Daniel Reinhardt talks from personal experience about social distance, dehumanization, and power as challenges to be addressed. A much-needed, thought-provoking look at a way forward."

Daniel Hahn, retired police chief

RETHINKING

AN OFFICER'S
CONFESSION
AND THE
PATHWAY
TO REFORM

THE
POLICE

DANIEL REINHARDT

An imprint of InterVarsity Press
Downers Grove, Illinois

InterVarsity Press
P.O. Box 1400 | Downers Grove, IL 60515-1426
ivpress.com | email@ivpress.com

InterVarsity Press® is the publishing division of InterVarsity Christian Fellowship/USA®. For more information, visit intervarsity.org.

Scripture quotations, unless otherwise noted, are from The Holy Bible, English Standard Version, copyright © 2001 by Crossway Bibles, a division of Good News Publishers. Used by permission. All rights reserved.

While any stories in this book are true, some names and identifying information may have been changed to protect the privacy of individuals.

The publisher cannot verify the accuracy or functionality of website URLs used in this book beyond the date of publication.

Cover design: David Fassett
Interior design: Daniel van Loon
Cover images: Getty Images: © natrot, © fotograzia, © Klubovy, © PaulMaguire

ISBN 978-1-5140-0612-2 (print) | ISBN 978-1-5140-0613-9 (digital)

Printed in the United States of America ∞

Library of Congress Cataloging-in-Publication Data
Names: Reinhardt, Daniel, 1974- author.
Title: Rethinking the police : an officer's confession and the pathway to
   reform / Daniel Reinhardt.
Description: Downers Grove, IL : InterVarsity Press, [2023] | Includes
   bibliographical references.
Identifiers: LCCN 2023019206 (print) | LCCN 2023019207 (ebook) | ISBN
   9781514006122 (paperback) | ISBN 9781514006139 (ebook)
Subjects: LCSH: Police–United States–History–21st century. | Police
   corruption–United States | Police brutality–United States. | Racism in
   law enforcement–United States.
Classification: LCC HV8139 .R45 2023 (print) | LCC HV8139 (ebook) | DDC
   363.20973–dc23/eng/20230606
LC record available at https://lccn.loc.gov/2023019206
LC ebook record available at https://lccn.loc.gov/2023019207

29 28 27 26 25 24 23 | 13 12 11 10 9 8 7 6 5 4 3 2 1

To the strongest person I know,

MY MOTHER,

who overcame cultural, economic, and oppressive
barriers through perseverance, integrity, and
character to become an educated woman of success.
Thank you for teaching me to value and love learning,
education, and the written word.

To our Lord and Savior be the glory!

CONTENTS

AWAKENING TO CULTURAL BLINDNESS

THE SONG "AMAZING GRACE" was written by the former slave-ship captain John Newton. He penned the famous words "I . . . was blind but now I see" nearly 250 years ago. When we consider the era in which it was written, perhaps the song expresses more than just a spiritual awakening. Surely Newton was influenced by his cultural context, where colonial slavery was an accepted norm. And he was not alone. Trapped by their cultural contexts, so many in that unfortunate period accepted the brutal and dehumanizing practices of colonial slavery without reserve.

We look back with horror, baffled at how our ancestors lived comfortably in the tension between a Christian culture and the insidious nature of slavery. Yet as perplexing as that era may be for modern observers, we must understand that culture can blind people to the truth whereby they participate in moral atrocities with a sense of justification. It is the unfortunate reality of humanity that we often accept the most egregious moral trespasses of our time.

"Amazing Grace," in a sense, is a song that celebrates not only spiritual freedom but also the freedom from the moral blindness of culture and race. It captures a slave-ship captain's radical shift from a deplorable agent of the slave trade to a passionate abolitionist. No longer blind to the darkness of his own heart nor the greatest injustice of his time, Newton had new eyes of grace to see beyond his own culturally enslaved perspective that perpetuated the enslavement of a people.

National cultures can vary based on racial identity. We all peer through lenses of diverse and racially influenced cultures and inherent biases. Consequently, we can miss what is painfully obvious to others who share a different racial and cultural context within the same nation. Frederick Douglass captured the grave nature of cultural distortion in nineteenth-century America:

> I have often been utterly astonished, since I came to the north, to find persons who could speak of the singing, among slaves, as evidence of their contentment and happiness. It is impossible to conceive of a greater mistake. Slaves sing most when they are most unhappy. The songs of the slave represent the sorrows of his heart; and he is relieved by them, only as an aching heart is relieved by its tears.[1]

So blinded by their culture, northern Whites mistook a song of longing and pain for an expression of contentment and joy. Drawing conclusions informed by their biases and culture, they could not have been more wrong. Yet Douglass was not trapped by such constraints. He deeply understood and felt the meaning of the songs:

> The hearing of those wild notes always depressed my spirit, and filled me with ineffable sadness. I have frequently found myself in tears while hearing them. The mere recurrence to those songs, even now, afflicts me; and while I am writing these lines, an expression of feeling has already found its way down my cheek.[2]

Through Douglass's speeches and writings, many White northerners had their blinders removed so they could truly see and understand the evil nature of slavery.

Yet racial and cultural bias did not disappear with the abolishment of slavery. Still today, we suffer the effects and struggle to understand the perspective of those quite different from us. So, of course, I too am blinded by my own culture. To understand my blindness and how I believe I've been freed—at least to some extent—first requires understanding my background.

I am a White male and was a police officer for twenty-four years in a racially diverse urban community. I was born and raised in the same community and lived most of my life in the city where I served. As a teenager, my high school had a dense population of African Americans. My wrestling team was coached by an African American man, and most of the athletes were African Americans. Although only a few White students earned spots on the team, I was fully welcomed and even loved. I developed friendships with my teammates, some of which have endured to the present day. After high school, I married an African American woman, and we have now been married for over twenty-eight years and have six children.

I am acquainted and even immersed to some extent in a diverse cultural context. I also have deep and meaningful relationships with African Americans. Yet sadly, neither my experiences nor my context freed me from the blindness and moral enslavement of police culture. For decades, I refused to accept what was painfully obvious for so many—police brutality against minorities is not an issue of a few isolated and disconnected incidents but a systemic condition of a compromised institution.

MY JOURNEY TO THE LIGHT

Prior to starting my PhD studies, I was an assistant pastor in an African American church in an impoverished area. The senior pastor had an abiding love for his people suffering from the effects of urban poverty. His mentorship helped free me from the influence of police culture, allowing me to witness the struggles and setbacks experienced by so many of my brothers and sisters during encounters with law enforcement. The congregation's gracious acceptance of my presence similarly humbled me, further tearing down my walls of apathy.

At this point in time, I began my research for my doctoral dissertation, a journey that began to peel away my blinders so I could see the light. Although enlightening, it was also difficult and painful. I gradually transitioned from nominal acknowledgment to substantial acceptance to passionate zeal for change. But my awakening was also predicated on experiences over twenty-four years—some quite traumatic—that helped me realize important factors paramount to the conclusions in this book. One early experience was particularly enlightening and, in hindsight, exposed the heart of the problem concerning police culture.

I began my law enforcement career at twenty-two years of age. I spent four months in the police academy, learning laws and standards of conduct as well as training in defensive tactics, driving, and firearms. The academy also indoctrinated me into a particular culture. For the most part, police academies are managed by police officers, and the training is shaped by the stories and experiences that the instructors tell. As a cadet, you're not just learning the curriculum, you're absorbing the officers' attitudes, vocabulary, and mannerisms, and the instructors are seasoned cops, which is the future every cadet hopes to achieve. I remember one instructor whose extensive experience in street crimes captivated me. As a young man, I admired him and hoped to be just like him. Looking back, I can see how my experience in the academy began to reshape my thinking, speech, and even who I perceived myself to be.

After the academy, I spent four months with training officers. Approximately eight months after I first walked in the door of the police department, I was on my own in a police cruiser. My grasp of the power I possessed did not run much deeper than a single, superficial thought: *I cannot believe they are letting me do this.* Within my first year of experience, I found myself involved in car chases and fights with suspects who resisted arrest. I was on the scene at bar brawls and arrived in the aftermath of rapes and murders. On one occasion, I witnessed an officer shot and later stood less than fifty feet away as two other officers killed the suspect. This was my new normal, yet I still had not meaningfully reflected on the implications. But then something happened during one of my night shifts that forced me to reckon with the power I possessed.

Domestic violence calls are common at night, but this one would turn out to be anything but. The female victim was screaming so loudly that the dispatchers could hear her as the neighbor across the street reported the incident from their front lawn. I was only a block away when I received the call, but my backup officer was blocked by a train. When I arrived at the residence, I could hear the visceral screaming, and I was alone.

I walked up the broken steps that led to the front door, which was open but obstructed by a screen. I pulled it open and stepped inside the residence. Ten feet away, I saw a couch facing the door where a woman crouched as an African American male loomed over her. They were involved in a struggle, and she was screaming. The motion of the man's arms and the intensity of the woman's screams made it clear to me that she was being stabbed. I unholstered my gun and pointed it at the man, yelling for him to stop and to get on the ground. Instead, he turned toward me. In less than a second, he had closed the space between the couch and the doorway, leaving me no time to retreat.

My academy training had taught me that deadly force was the appropriate response to a knife attack. I knew that I could not stop him with my left hand alone, but I had no time to holster my weapon to free my right for self-defense. So I took the slack out of the trigger, preparing to fire.

But I never pulled the trigger.

For reasons that I could not explain at the time, I chose instead to grab the young man's right hand with my left hand, knowing full well it wouldn't be enough to stop the knife. To my surprise, he didn't resist. I turned him toward the wall and handcuffed him. Still there was no resistance. Finally, I turned him around to secure his knife.

It wasn't there.

Despite my certainty seconds earlier, there was no knife, and there never had been.

Once I realized he was weaponless, I asked him, "Why didn't you listen to me? Why didn't you get on the ground?"

With anger and utter sincerity, he yelled, "I'm tired of her! I came out so you could take me to jail."

I walked the man down the front steps I had crossed only a few moments earlier and placed him in the rear of my police cruiser. When I sat down in the driver's seat, my hands began to tremble, but not because of stress or concern that my life had been in danger. I was used to those feelings by that point. Instead, I trembled at the realization that I nearly killed a man who had no intention to harm me.

For many years, I couldn't explain why I never pulled the trigger and ended that young man's life. My choice was completely inconsistent with my training. I was fully convinced that he was about to stab me and knew I couldn't stop him by grabbing his hand. More than twenty years later, I now see that my faith was a key part of my response. Because I believed that young man was intrinsically valuable and created in God's image, I valued his life. My values countered my training, tipping the scales in that encounter, and I am forever thankful they did.

Here's what I've learned from that call and other experiences over two decades of law enforcement:

Police culture matters. Police officers are shaped by police culture, and that internal culture is present in every experience and every encounter they have as officers.

Internal culture shapes the ways police officers use force. If the culture does not promote valuing people and relationships within the community, the exercise of power—and specifically the use of force—can have catastrophic consequences.

Change is not impossible. Influences both within officers and in the culture of their department can reshape police officers and reorient the choices that they make.

The police will continue to use force, and officers will be in in situations like the one I described where their choice is literally a matter of life and death. Unfortunately, this is a consequence of living in a fallen world. We cannot change that reality; however, we can take meaningful steps to ensure officers are shaped in a way that truly promotes valuing the lives of people—particularly people of color.

THE URGENCY OF THIS MOMENT

Throughout the history of American policing, racial minorities—African Americans in particular—have experienced the catastrophic consequences of a culture that has inconsistently valued their lives.[3] As a result, there is tension with and mistrust of the police in many African American communities.[4] Repeated tragedies in the years following the 2014 death of Michael Brown in Ferguson, Missouri, have increased public awareness of this tension.[5] In his 2015 book, *Copping Out*, Anthony Stanford explains,

> The Ferguson incident and its aftermath have focused attention on the chasm between young black males and police across the country. . . . Tense protests, exasperation, and racially explosive situations related to the deaths of unarmed black males such as Michael Brown, Trayvon Martin, and Eric Garner have become a catalyst to examine the treatment of black males by law enforcement organizations.[6]

In the years since Stanford wrote those words, the antipathy has only grown greater. In 2020, the tensions seemed to reach a breaking point.

On February 23, 2020, a former police officer and his son shot and killed Ahmaud Arbery, a Black male who was jogging in their neighborhood. Less than a month later, the Louisville Police Department executed a no-knock warrant on a residence where neither of their intended suspects turned out to have been present, and Breonna Taylor, a twenty-six-year-old African American woman who worked as a medical technician, was shot to death. Ten days after Taylor's death, Daniel Prude, an African American man who suffered from mental health issues, died of asphyxiation when police officers in Rochester, New York, placed a bag over his head and held him on the ground. Two months later, a Minneapolis police officer knelt for eight minutes on George Floyd's neck, resulting in his death from a heart attack. Six months after the death of Breonna Taylor, a grand jury failed to indict any of the officers who had unleashed a hail of gunfire in her apartment for murder. Only one officer was indicted on three charges of wanton endangerment. The result in Louisville was a wave of demonstrations in which two police officers were shot.

Reflecting on the death of Michael Brown and others, as well as the events in 2020, many may have attributed the problem of police brutality to a few racist officers; however, the death of Tyre Nichols in 2023 at the hands of five African American police officers shattered that paradigm. Perhaps the pain and confusion are greater than ever before.

How should people feel, particularly African Americans, when faced with such an onslaught? In her book *The Case for Rage: Why Anger Is Essential to Anti-Racist Struggle*, Myisha Cherry explains the grief, frustration, and rage many African Americans are experiencing in this tumultuous period. Just as important, she underscores why the current context demands a response: "The connection between anger and racial justice is maybe more at the top of more readers' minds than it would have been in 2019 or any year before, as protests and other activism reached a crescendo across the United States when many could no longer hold inside their anger at police violence."[7] Cherry represents the sentiment of many Americans from varying demographics, and as an African American woman, she understands the deep reservoir of emotion that weighs on her community regarding the police—they simply cannot hold it in any longer.

Like Cherry, I believe action must be taken. We cannot continue with casual passivity in the face of mounting tensions and violence. Cherry, however, writes from an unapologetically secular perspective with clearly perceived presuppositions tied to Marxism, evolutionary scientism, and other non-Christian perspectives. Her solutions are not neutral but inextricably formed by the presuppositions that guide her analysis. Although I value her work and resonate with her intentions, she analyzes the problem from what I believe to be erroneous foundational presuppositions, underscoring the need for an authentic Christian analysis to an urgent problem. Additionally, Tyre Nichols's tragic death, more so perhaps than the other cases, calls for more than just a Christian response. It demands a Christian response that deeply and intimately understands the true nature of policing and police culture.

THE NEGLECTED FACTOR IN THE PROBLEM OF POLICE BRUTALITY

Local law enforcement agencies, courts, and federal agencies are not blind to the problem of police brutality and misuse of force.[8] In fact, there have been many attempts to deal with this issue through external reforms,[9] though they have not resulted in lasting change.[10] The problems remain, and African Americans sense that little progress has been made following the changes that arose from the civil rights movement.[11]

So what has been missed?

Past reforms have tended to focus on external factors and failed to effectively face the internal factors.[12] For instance, some Supreme Court decisions and Presidential Crime Commissions have attempted to restrain and reform the police by addressing specific practices or external factors. However, these measures have never truly cultivated meaningful and lasting reform.[13] When I refer to "internal factors," I'm describing the culture, worldview, and implicit social structures of law enforcement agencies.[14] The public must begin to recognize such internal factors to apply pressure to law enforcement leaders to address the internal cultural structures that contribute to the problem of police brutality against racial minorities. This doesn't mean external factors don't also contribute to police brutality or that internal factors have been completely ignored; they simply have not been sufficiently addressed.[15]

My research has identified three key internal factors that shape cultures that perpetuate police brutality:

Social distance. The police possess a social identity that tends to be distinct and different from the social identity of racial minorities.[16] As a result of the disparity, police struggle to relate to racial minorities in a personal and respectful manner, at times even perceiving themselves as superior to the community.[17]

Unchecked power. Police possess significant power, and the social structures of police departments shape the behavior within in ways that fail to place appropriate limits on this power.[18] Misdirected or misused power coupled with social distance multiplies proclivities for abuse.[19]

Social structures that reinforce negative perceptions of minorities. The combination of distance and power opens the door for dehumanization directed toward particular racial and ethnic groups.

WHAT MAKES THIS BOOK UNIQUE AND NEEDED?

This book captures my research journey linking police culture to systemic racism and police brutality, underscoring the need to address internal factors. I understand many outside of policing have argued extensively for the existence of systemic racism in policing. However, I believe this book is unique for a few important reasons.

First, it offers the perspective of a police officer—not an outside observer—who walked the road from skepticism to a demand for change. Second, while culture and systemic racism are often presented as opposing explanations to a problem or disparity,[20] I will detail how police leadership, organizational structure, culture, and ethics organically support a particular strategy that ensures disproportionate enforcement and an enhanced proclivity for abuse in the form of police brutality. My research will demonstrate how internal factors stemming from police culture are powerful forces contributing to police brutality and biased policing. Third, the evidence I will present is supported by both research and firsthand experience. Lastly, this book will not just expose the problem, but will offer a pathway to change beyond recommending better practices alone.

That said, the pathway to change I will argue for entails a specific leadership model and ethic structured to impact police culture. Until police culture changes, police practices will not substantially change. The culture is the heart feeding the systemically racist strategies. Thus, the heart—police culture—is the target for the transformation so that community-friendly strategies can grow beyond nominal support to become wholeheartedly implemented.[21]

YOUR JOURNEY

For the reader who raises an eyebrow at the term *systemic racism*, I am aware many scholars and writers assume systemic racism and oppression based solely on the statistical disparities between racial minorities and White Americans. Certainly, these disparities could be due to systemic racism, but the disparities alone are not sufficient evidence to support a case for systemic racism, a fact I believe Thomas Sowell has labored thoroughly and established definitively.[22] But I will not argue for systemic racism based solely on statistical disparity. Instead, I will establish clear evidence accounting for the disparity that suggests systemic racism. Also, by *systemic racism*, I do not mean laws or legal sanctions that are explicitly racist. Rather, I have in mind a form of racism that is often implicit, disguised, and embedded in social structures where the intentions of people can be good and perhaps not even remotely racist:

> Racism is not always conscious, explicit, or readily visible—often it is systemic and structural. Systemic and structural racism are forms of racism that are pervasively and deeply embedded in systems, laws, written or unwritten policies, and entrenched practices and beliefs that produce, condone, and perpetuate widespread unfair treatment and oppression of people of color.[23]

I will present clear evidence of "unwritten policies" and "entrenched practices and beliefs" that are "deeply embedded" in the social structure of law enforcement that support a seemingly innocuous police strategy that is truly systemically racist, ensuring "unfair treatment and oppression" for communities of color.

For the reader who raises an eyebrow at the Christian emphasis, as I will explain later in the book, although the leadership model I present is distinctly Christian, it is in no way ecclesiastical. In other words, although there is certainly a Christian philosophical undergirding, the model is in no way designed for a spiritual application or context. The model is specifically designed for a secular police context.

Additionally, a Christian leadership philosophy is helpful given the current context for two reasons. First, policing, like so many other institutions in America, was formed by Christian presuppositions.[24] In the West this reality is likely unavoidable to some extent. As the agnostic scholar Tom Holland argues in his book *Dominion*, the Christian worldview and ethic has invaded all Western culture, including the movements that objected to the Christian faith. Thus, a Christian emphasis for leadership and ethics is organic to the foundations of policing.

Second, Christianity is not only foundational to American policing but shares a dynamic relationship with secular culture. H. Richard Niebuhr posited five differing relationships between Christianity and culture and seemed to support a relationship between the two that emphasized the transformative power of Christianity to unethical aspects of secular culture.[25] D. A. Carson, analyzing Niebuhr, advocates for a more holistic approach rather than a categorical one. However, he also recognizes the mandate for the faith to transform culture.[26] Christianity, therefore, is not only foundational to policing but also integrative and transformative by nature, making it a natural philosophical leadership foundation for transforming a compromised culture.

My hope is that readers from all backgrounds will take this journey with optimism. Although police brutality has plagued communities for over a century and the tension between racial minorities and the police appears to be worsening, I believe there is real hope for reform and redemption in law enforcement. Please remember, I was fully indoctrinated by a culture that enslaved me to a skewed and dangerous perspective. I am not merely an academic observer. I have tasted and seen police culture in all its sophistication and nuances. I can truly say, "I was blind, but now I see," and I fully believe if more people are given the same visibility, we can advocate for change and reform in law enforcement together.

For the readers who love and support the police, know that I do too! Please do not misunderstand me in the pages ahead. I am not in favor of defunding the police or arguing that policing is a dishonorable profession. Nor am I arguing that police are the sole reason behind the tension with communities of color or that urban violence is an overblown problem. I realize the journey will not be easy for some, but my hope is that you will weigh the evidence and transition from skepticism to passionate zeal for the redemption of policing. To my fellow officers, my brothers and sisters in blue, although you may not agree with me, please do not doubt my genuine love for the men and woman who serve their communities. I come from within and am unashamed to count myself as one of you.

PART 1

DRIFTING AWAY
FROM PEACE
TOWARD ABUSE
AND BRUTALITY

CHAPTER 1

A HISTORY OF THE POLICE

FROM PROMISING
BEGINNINGS TO ABUSE

THROUGHOUT MY TWENTY-FOUR-YEAR career as a police officer, I was thanked for my service on many occasions. In restaurants and drive-thrus, I often went to pay my bill only to learn an unknown person already paid it. Gestures like these are not necessarily based on anything an individual officer has done, but due to the recognition that an officer is part of a collective. A police officer represents a history and culture over 150 years old. During that time, many officers have served honorably, and some have even paid the ultimate price by dying in the line of duty. People recognize and appreciate these sacrifices by honoring representatives of the collective.

Most officers readily accept the gratitude and truly appreciate the sentiment. We love advancing this noble history, even though the kindness we receive may not directly relate to anything specific we have done. I believe this is a healthy attitude, and all officers should accept the compliment stemming from the connection with our history.

However, we should also take the bad with the good.

When the public recognizes our past of racism and abuse, officers tend to shy away from any association with these negative realities. Acknowledging our participation in the enforcement of Jim Crow laws and other disturbing practices of the past is difficult. Yet our history cannot be disconnected from who we are. Today, we can view video of officers wading into masses of peaceful African American protestors during the civil rights movement and beating them with batons. We are part of that history too. The uniform I wore every day represented the entire story—which is not an easy truth to digest. When these unfortunate events in our history are brought to light, officers tend to respond by noting they weren't alive when these things took place, or that they aren't the perpetrators of the incidents of brutality taking place today.

I understand the tendency to reject our past failures and accept only the honorable aspects of law enforcement. But we are representatives of a history and culture in all that it is and is not—the amazing acts of valor and the despicable abuses. We represent both those who gave their lives in service and those who abused their power. If we adopt an incomplete and inaccurate depiction of our history, we will cease to truly know who we are as a profession, a culture, and a people—the "family" of law enforcement, as we like to say.

THE JOURNEY FROM PEEL AND PEACE TO TENSION AND ABUSE

The modern idea of policing started with a Christian foundation, oriented toward servanthood, the cultivation of peace, and the judicious exercise of power. However, almost immediately the

American police deviated from this philosophical foundation. Understanding the drift from this foundation into the sad history of abuses and reforms will help the reader appreciate how police culture was formed.

While serving as the British Home Secretary, Sir Robert Peel created a modern police force in London in 1829. It emphasized peacekeeping and later served as the model for the first modern police forces in the United States.[1] He drafted nine foundational principles focused on the prevention of crime, public approval and respect, public cooperation, the judicious use of force, impartial service to all members of society, friendliness, strong public relations, police unity with the public, and professionalism.[2] Robert Peel's principles reflected one foundational maxim: "To keep the peace by peaceful means."[3]

Peel was a Christian, and his principles were a reaction, at least to some extent, to the objections of evangelical Christians concerning law enforcement practices. "British evangelicals long had protested Britain's legal and penal system; its law enforcement strategy involved tactics that some citizens found intimidating. . . . Peel was sympathetic to these evangelicals."[4] The principles he drafted were partly a response to the concerns of these British evangelicals and became the foundation for American police departments promoting peace and harmony. That foundation, however, would not hold for long.

1845–1960: THE BEGINNINGS OF CORRUPTION AND REFORM

In 1845, New York City was the first modern police department built on Peel's principles.[5] However, the model for police in the

United States differed from that of London in that they were municipal and not federal, thus controlled by local politicians, and even at this point known to be "more liberal in their use of force than were the English bobbies."[6] The police became tools in the hands of politicians and subject to their agendas, which led to selective enforcement by law enforcement and politicians taking bribes to reward positions in the police departments.[7] Sadly, despite the promise of Peel's foundation, modern policing in America was imperiled from the start.

Nonetheless, there were some promising aspects of early policing. For instance, the police tended to be heavily involved in social services. The Boston Police Department, for example, housed the homeless, while the New York Police Department entertained children at the police stations, looked after troubled youth, and started a "junior police program."[8] Police officers served their communities through more relational functions and were not simply focused on criminal enforcement.

However, in the 1930s reform efforts shifted the focus away from such services as corruption continued to worsen throughout the 1920s, prompting President Hoover to form a commission in response. The Wickersham Commission published the *Report on Lawlessness in Law Enforcement*, which detailed how the police utilized "intimidation, brutality, illegal arrests and detention," particularly when interacting with "particular groups of people such as racial and ethnic minorities."[9] Sadly, it only took American police departments a matter of decades to become thoroughly corrupt and brutal.[10]

By the 1930s, the need for police reform was glaring, and was instituted through more science-based policing, where the police focused on professional conduct, enforcement of criminal law, criminal investigation, and objective hiring practices.[11] Reform efforts eventually wrestled control from corrupt local politicians and gave authority to police chiefs, who provided structure and accountability for officers.[12] Additionally, motorized patrol increased an officer's range and the ability of supervisors to oversee officers in the field. However, motorized patrol also had the adverse effect of separating officers from their communities.[13] The reforms of the 1930s helped reduce police corruption, but the focus on crime fighting and motorized patrol further contributed to the dwindling of social services, distancing the officer from the community.

Sir Robert Peel had conceived of police success as an absence of crime, not the presence of enforcement. Police departments in the United States, however, deviated from Peel's principles and measured success through arrests and other crime statistics. Gaines, Kappeler, and Vaughn describe the 1940s and 1950s as a professional phase in policing and provide a helpful description:

> The professional phase of policing produced a more efficient police organization that was devoted to criminal apprehension. Officers were moved from foot patrol to vehicular patrol and a variety of technologies were adopted. Police officers were discouraged from getting involved with citizens for fear of breeding corruption. Also, efficiency of operation was considered more important than solving problems, and the application of human

relation skills within the police organization or by its officers in their daily activities was viewed as being inefficient and therefore unprofessional.[14]

Even at this early stage of American policing, one can clearly see the drift away from community relationships, problem solving, and crime prevention toward impersonal enforcement. Police departments were crime-focused and insulated from outside control, but while their autonomy lessened corruption among the ranks, it also removed them from external accountability.[15] The 1940s and 1950s also surfaced growing tensions among mostly White police departments toward racial minorities, even while garnering support among the middle class.[16]

The modern American police department may have been inspired by London's police force and Peel's nine principles, but it swiftly embraced a more liberal use of force. Amid the influence of local corruption and reform efforts, police continued to deviate from Peel's principles, focusing on crime and enforcement of criminal violations rather than community relations and peacekeeping. Technology, the emphasis on more science-based policing, and professionalism further contributed to officers isolating themselves from the community. The social distance was most poignant in communities of color, and the tensions between mostly White police departments and African Americans took root in the decades leading up to the 1960s.[17] The history of policing in America has been one of ever-increasing social distance, particularly with racial minorities, where tensions were growing in communities of color throughout the decades following the Second World War.

1960–1990: TURBULENCE AND CHANGE

The simmering pot came to a boil in the 1960s.[18] The war in Vietnam, the increase of crime, the civil rights movement, and the assassinations of John Kennedy, Martin Luther King Jr., and Robert Kennedy marked this decade as one of severe turbulence, and the police were not prepared to deal with the new challenges.[19] The 1960s "shocked" and "changed" the police, and riots, crime commissions, and Supreme Court decisions were instrumental factors in the process.[20]

In 1965, the arrest of an African American driver sparked a riot in Watts, a neighborhood in Los Angeles, resulting in several deaths and extensive property damage. Over the next three years, numerous riots occurred in other US cities,[21] including the 1968 riot in Chicago at the Democratic National Convention. Media coverage of the event made the reality of police brutality harder to ignore. Excessive force was no longer hidden in the dark alleys of urban ghettos but was now fully displayed on the television sets in middle-class White living rooms across America.[22]

In 1967, President Johnson created the Commission on Law Enforcement and Administration of Justice. The commission made several recommendations, but its most important contribution was in noting that "community relations . . . were especially strained in minority communities," and identifying the need for "improved community relations" and "the need to recruit minority officers."[23] Additionally, President Johnson appointed the Kerner Commission in 1968 to investigate the causes, occurrences, and potential solutions to the riots.[24] This commission arrived at a similar conclusion, but expressed the problem with greater clarity. Vila and Morris explain, "The main conclusion reached by the commission in its report disseminated in 1968, was that 'Our nation is moving toward two societies, one black and one white—separate and unequal.'"[25] Additionally, the commission determined that the racial divide was a serious problem between police officers and minorities in impoverished communities, and the hostility between the groups was contributing to the tension and violence.[26]

Time and again, the crime commissions of the 1960s concluded that police action during the decade's riots demonstrated police brutality, which further heightened hostility between the police and African Americans in impoverished communities.

This decade also included three significant Supreme Court rulings that impacted the operations of the police: *Mapp v. Ohio* (1961); *Miranda v. Arizona* (1966); and *Terry v. Ohio* (1968). The first two limited police power by excluding evidence from prosecution that was obtained illegally by the police and ensuring victims were read their rights before custodial interrogations.[27] *Terry v. Ohio*, however, formally expanded police power by extending the right for police to stop and frisk people who appear suspicious, even if they have not committed a crime.[28]

Perhaps most challenging for police was the anti-establishment mindset of the 1960s. In the early twentieth century, students formed socialist groups, focusing on issues related to higher education and the World Wars.[29] By the 1960s a "New Left" had emerged with a similar agenda focusing on the war in Vietnam, social and racial issues, and authority structures.[30] Herbert Marcuse had a significant impact on this movement, arguing that free speech does not lead to change because of the lack of power. Therefore, the voices of those in power should be silenced, or at least reduced—even by force—or those without power will never be heard.[31] Consequently, many rejected their parents' values, worldview, and the established norms set by preceding generations.[32]

Despite the focus on peace, the protests and actions of the younger generation precipitated violence.[33] The dynamic, changing world of the 1960s, oppositional mindsets against society, and the criminal justice system as a whole presented the police with difficult challenges.[34] These factors certainly contributed to the outbreak of violence in this turbulent decade. Nonetheless, police brutality still became a recognized problem, and leaders in law enforcement understood the real need to provide solutions,[35] which fueled a new interest in law enforcement research that led to new findings in the 1970s that led to new police strategies in the 1980s.[36] Finally, the police began to understand the need for problem-oriented policing and cooperation with citizens, and new philosophies of policing would set the stage for community policing in the 1990s.[37] Unfortunately, after the events of September 11, 2001, policing once again embraced an enforcement-centric strategy, and authentic community policing faded and dwindled.[38]

Nonetheless, as forward progress took place in the criminal justice system during the latter half of the twentieth century, public notice waned toward law enforcement's use of excessive force. That all changed, however, after an event in the early 1990s brought police brutality back into the living rooms of America and captured the attention of the country once again.

1990–2023: INCREASING TENSION AND AWARENESS

In 1991, Rodney King led the Los Angeles Police Department on a vehicle pursuit until he was eventually apprehended. During his arrest, King was tasered and beaten repeatedly with batons. The incident drew national attention because it was captured on video and led to local rioting and civil unrest.[39] Once again, America was unable to look away. The conjecture and rumors of police brutality were now on full display for all to see, with tangible evidence supporting the claims of generations of people of color. It simply could not be dismissed, nor could the civil unrest that followed.

The resulting Christopher Commission found that policing needed reform, and its recommendations not only fueled change throughout the Los Angeles police but resulted in reforms in law enforcement nationwide.[40] Yet despite the efforts and progress, incidents of police brutality continued, receiving national attention from the late nineties and into the twenty-first century. In 1997, Abner Louima, a Haitian immigrant, was assaulted and sodomized with a toilet plunger by the police.[41] Additionally, the controversial 2006 police shooting of Sean Bell, an African American man, reached national headlines.[42] These cases and many others illustrate that, despite the reform sparked by the Christopher Commission, police brutality against racial minorities, especially African American males, remained a grave problem.

In the last decade, the issue of police brutality has become a matter of serious public concern.[43] Several incidents have ignited the long-standing tension between the police and racial minorities, specifically African Americans, leading to civil unrest and violent protests.[44] The year 2014 bore witness to four particularly horrific events: Michael Brown, unarmed at the time, was shot and killed by a White police officer in Ferguson, Missouri; Eric Garner died from a choke hold applied by a White police officer in New York; Ezell Ford, also unarmed, was shot and killed by Los Angeles police officers; and twelve-year-old Tamir Rice was shot and killed by a White Cleveland police officer while holding a pellet gun. Then in 2015, Freddie Gray died from a crushed voice box and spinal injuries at a hospital after being taken into custody by Baltimore police officers.[45] Each of the victims was an African American male.

And then came 2020.

Amid a pandemic and a polarizing presidential election, the deaths of Breonna Taylor, Daniel Prude, and George Floyd triggered a wave of nationwide protests and widespread civil unrest. Additionally, the "defund the police" movement emerged, as well as growing support for the Black Lives Matter movement, both clearly related to the mistrust of the police emanating from encounters between White police officers and people of color.

As many were still trying to reckon with the racial implications of 2020 concerning the police and African Americans, in 2023 communities were confronted with the disturbing video of Tyre Nichols's death at the hands of five African American police officers. More will be said later on this, once I explain the police culture and its influence; but for now, what can we conclude from this brief survey? The tension between the police and communities of color is at an all-time high, and despite the move away from corruption in the 1930s and the meaningful external reforms in the 1970s through the 1990s, incidents of police brutality continued and may have even increased. Why? Because despite the steady move away from corruption and needed external reforms, an internal factor remained at work decade after decade. The police were steadily drifting away from the public socially, particularly in communities of color. The catastrophic consequences of this ever-growing social distance will be highlighted in the next chapter as we explore police culture.

CHAPTER 2

POLICE CULTURE

SOCIAL DISTANCE, DEHUMANIZATION, AND ABUSE

MY LAW ENFORCEMENT CAREER began not long after the arrest of Rodney King. I watched the LAPD take him into custody before I was an officer. I think anyone who viewed the attack would conclude it was exactly that—an attack. However, as a new police officer, I discovered officers saw the incident differently. The focus of conversation was not on abuse, but on how the LAPD foolishly allowed the footage of the incident to enter circulation. Nearly every officer I encountered considered King a criminal who got what he deserved. If he had not led the LAPD on a vehicle pursuit and resisted arrest, the aftermath would have never occurred.

Officers understood that the encounter between the LAPD and King affected police departments across the country. It became the impetus for nationwide changes in police use of force training, even where I served in Ohio. Many senior officers were disgruntled over the new training guidelines.

For years they had carried two tools considered extremely effective: a blackjack and a billy club. A blackjack had a short handle with a heavy golf ball–sized lead ball at the end and was generally used in close-quarter struggles. The billy club, or straight stick, was used when the person resisting was at arm's length. For decades these officers aimed each of these tools at one target—the head. Generally, when a person gets jacked or clubbed in the head, they stop resisting, either due to capitulation or unconsciousness.

Stories regularly circulated about the old days when officers competed over the effectiveness of their technique, the winner being whoever's bludgeoned arrestee received the most stitches at the hospital. As an officer, I never witnessed an incident like this, and many of the stories were perhaps exaggerated. But the undeniable truth is that these stories were told to cast the abusive officers as heroes, not villains. I wish I could say I was appalled by the stories when I first heard them, but sadly I cannot. Like so many officers, I had been indoctrinated into a dangerous cultural mindset.

Regardless of the "glorious past," all officers—including senior officers—understood that violent measures like these were no longer acceptable. Public backlash from the treatment of Rodney King had changed training around police force. We were taught humane ways to effect an arrest on a resistive or combative person and received new tools designed to end conflicts reasonably rather than render people unconscious. Training emphasized targeting areas of the body that would not cause permanent damage or pose a risk of serious injury, unconsciousness, or death to the person.

Continuums for force were stressed to govern when and how aggressively the tools could be used against people who resisted arrest. We had to consider the person's level of resistance and then respond with a reasonable application of force to counter the resistance. While this process was the correct approach for a police officer, it was not as simple or "effective" as the old way, as it required an officer to think quickly and respond humanely. The changes required more thought and effort and increased the onus of accountability.

One of the new tools introduced was the expandable baton. It was lighter and smaller than a billy club and was designed for use on areas like the legs, arms, and shoulders. Displeased with the tool, some officers began carrying large flashlights made of steel and loaded with large, heavy batteries. This became the new billy club, disguised as a flashlight. The updated training guidelines also failed to account for an easy workaround, as officers committed to targeting an arrestee's head could simply write in their report that they swung at the person's shoulder, but the arrestee ducked, hence the head wound.

Whatever external reforms come along, police culture is the engine driving the application and practices of officers at the street level. External changes can only do so much when police culture has the power to resist and even reverse their efforts. This chapter will detail the specifics of police culture so the reader may understand why this is undeniably so.

DRIFTING AWAY FROM HUMANITY AND COMPASSION

For many police departments, SWAT officers are the epitome of what an officer should be. The SWAT (Special Weapons and

Tactics) team reflects police culture in its most intense form. Those deemed heroes of the police department end up on the SWAT team, and it wasn't long before I wanted to be ranked among them, a desire I achieved in my third year of service.

Generally, the SWAT team is involved in more dangerous police operations, like serving no-knock warrants on drug houses and calls involving barricaded gunmen. It's also one of the most militarized units in the police force. We raided drug houses wearing black hoods that covered our faces, while carrying automatic rifles. The SWAT team's operations are not only dangerous, they're also the most impersonal. You are a nameless, black-hooded figure storming into citizens' homes with aggression and tactical precision. We threw flash-bangs through windows while simultaneously breaking down doors with a ram. Fourteen officers blitzed into a residence pointing rifles in the faces of terrified people while screaming, "Get on the ground! Police search warrant!" Few people resist such a sudden, dramatic, and terrifying experience, instead stopping dead in their tracks with looks of horror frozen on their faces.

SWAT operations are certainly dangerous, and the tactics involved are intended to protect life, but it's hard to exercise compassion during this type of operation. Within my first year on the team, I began to struggle with my new duties. The utter terror in people's eyes as we invaded their homes grated at my moral convictions. Some of those we arrested were engaged in violent criminal activity, and we did our best to avoid raiding a house while innocents were present, but it was often unavoidable. And the memory of a terror-stricken weeping toddler is hard to erase from your mind.

I believe many officers simply disconnect from this reality to avoid the tension caused by the inhumanity inherent to the work. It's natural to gravitate toward self-defense mechanisms. Some of my brothers on the SWAT team regularly referred to the people we encountered during raids as rats—even the children. That said, I'd caution against reacting in anger and demonizing these men outright. I knew them. They were devoted husbands, loving fathers, and men of integrity in other arenas of their life. But they had been shaped by police culture, and the disparity of their character likely never entered their mind.

Soldiers are indoctrinated into the military through basic training, some of them going on to enter combat. These two short-term experiences can transform their lives forever. An officer's experience within police culture does not resemble such a sudden change. It's more like a slow poison or erosion. Year after year, an officer slowly becomes more distant, more prone to dehumanize, possibly even abusive. Of course, some officers remain more resilient than others and weather the stress of policing, police culture, and the horrific tragedies they encounter on a regular basis in a positive manner, but no one is immune.

This seems demonstrable in the lack of empathy toward the Black Lives Matter movement by the Blue Lives Matter movement. Blue Lives Matter was birthed after the protests following the death of Michael Brown, and its contentious nature toward Black Lives Matter is clearly evident on its website: "The media catered to movements such as Black Lives Matter, whose goal was the vilification of law enforcement."[1]

According to this perspective, Black Lives Matter was an assault on the very character of the police.

Michael Brown's death, however, was not a standalone incident, but one of many acts of violence occurring in the greater context of a long history of abuse and brutality by police. Detaching it from this historical context is myopic, leading to a narrow understanding of the situation that ignores the pain and anguish felt by many African Americans over Brown's death. I believe the police in general had a difficult time understanding Black Lives Matter, at least as a statement, holistically and contextually, and didn't respond with empathy or compassion. Given the timing of Blue Lives Matter's origin, one would be hard pressed to depict their response as anything but confrontational. The police didn't grasp the offense of their response. However, it was not a standalone occurrence. It is anchored to a history of abuse where police culture is the mainstay, the shaping power of which ensures the same result: racial minorities victimized by the police.

POLICE DEPARTMENTS AS SOCIAL STRUCTURES

Police officers are not autonomous agents acting in a vacuum. They exist and operate not only in the broader culture but also within a social structure—the police department. Although social structures are formed by people, they are nonetheless "ontologically real," and they influence those who operate within them.[2] A person's decisions will reflect the boundaries and guidelines represented by their social structure.[3] People are aware of the guidelines, restraints, and incentives, and these realities influence, restrain, and guide behavior.[4]

For example, the social structure of a university places no restraints on an eighteen-year-old student and a twenty-two-year-old student dating. However, that of a high school prohibits an eighteen-year-old student from dating a twenty-two-year-old teacher. The differing roles create two completely different guidelines for ethical conduct. Clearly, social structures influence people's conscience and moral behavior.[5] Skolnick and Fyfe explain, "Police do not make their choices by a rational calculation. . . . Choices are made instead on moral grounds, developed within the subculture of a police department."[6] Since police departments are social structures, they provide guidelines that shape the moral parameters and rules for a new officer.

What does this look like at the practical level? When an officer pulls over an off-duty officer for speeding, the "right" thing to do is to let your brother or sister officer off with a warning. Enforcing the law dispassionately is simply inappropriate if not downright wrong in this situation. Why? Because the officer is making this moral decision in and not apart from the values instilled by the police culture of the police department. Citizens—who obviously operate outside the police culture—view this action differently, interpreting the warning as unmerited preferential treatment and, therefore, immoral. From the citizen's perspective, the people who enforce the traffic laws should be the last ones to violate the law and if anything, should be held to a greater degree of accountability.

But officers see it differently. Police culture teaches them that they are above the people and the law. (This will be explained in greater detail later.) I suspect most officers would categorically reject my claim, but only because they have not thought it through. A few years before I retired, an officer from a department outside of the jurisdiction where I served pulled over one of my colleagues as he was leaving an establishment that served alcohol and ended up arresting him for driving while intoxicated. The event caused an uproar among us, with some on the force furious at our chief for not speaking out against this "unrighteous action."

Worst of all, the character of the arresting officer was maligned, and he was thoroughly demonized, characterized as an unethical traitor who committed an unforgiveable offense. I know him personally, and this depiction of him was completely distorted and untrue. He is an honorable man of integrity who was simply doing his duty. Nonetheless, police culture shapes officers in such a way that they may not even recognize the irony of the moral convictions they embrace, and those who go against the cultural moral code face serious social repercussions. The police department is a powerful instrument of ethical formation.

All subcultures are formative, but they are not all the same. A unique phenomenon occurs within the police subculture in that police have an informal code that can differ significantly from the formal code that is, at least outwardly, supported by management.[7] The informal aspect of the subculture is often where the ethically dubious behavior is found, like police brutality.[8] What is passed informally from officer to officer may not only contradict the formal guidelines and procedures, but may also have more influential power on officers' actions than the official guidelines and procedures.[9] More often than not, the informal subculture of the police becomes the norm and true guideline for procedures at the street level.[10]

Those who think they can grasp the cultural values of police departments through formal training structures, policy manuals, and mission statements are grossly misguided. In fact, such points of study may be the very antithesis of the cultural heart of the department. Police culture is the true author of department values.

SOCIAL IDENTITY, SOCIAL DISTANCE, AND DEHUMANIZATION

The social identity of the police is foundationally related to how the police view themselves and how they view and relate to the community. As a result, it is an important consideration related to the problem of police brutality and morally upright policing. One particularly concerning aspect is how police officers tend to see themselves as pitted against the rest of society and feel that only other officers can be trusted. Malcolm D. Holmes and Brad W. Smith explain that the police have an "us-them" worldview, and "they divide the world into two camps—fellow officers who can be trusted, and others who cannot. . . . In the extreme, the police believe that most of society is against them."[11] This social identity leads to social isolation and, consequently, social distance from the community.[12]

The us-them worldview in police interactions with racial minorities is an important consideration concerning the fact that police detainment and deadly force is disproportionally higher among racial minorities, and specifically African American men.[13] Related to the disproportionality, studies reveal that when the police perceive people to have poor attitudes, they are more likely to use force.[14] Further complicating the matter, racial minorities tend to view the police with suspicion and fear.[15] These factors collide in a perfect storm anytime police stop and detain racial minorities at a disproportionate rate and are likely to perceive their attitudes as less than compliant in light of the fear and distrust toward law enforcement. These frequent encounters can cause the police to stereotype an entire group and view racial minorities, particularly African Americans, as threats to themselves and the peace of the community.[16]

Further exacerbating the problem is the racial disparity among police officers. Most police officers in America are White, middle-class males, and this holds true even in communities with higher percentages of racial minorities.[17] The racial divide and failure of middle-class White Americans to relate constructively to racial minorities exists in the context of majority White police forces that serve communities of color.[18] The clash of worldviews and identities contributes to conflict and incidents of police brutality and biased policing.

Social distance and stereotyping are factors of concern related to police culture. Equally concerning is the tendency for officers to dehumanize racial minorities. Jack L. Colwell and Charles Huth explain,

> This type of "class distinction" [us versus them] serves to widen the gap between the police and the communities they patrol. Officers feel more comfortable distancing themselves from subjects mentally, physically, and

emotionally, which permits them to dehumanize the most challenging clientele, but inevitably dehumanizes everyone geographically or racially associated.[19]

An officer's social identity isolates and distances them from their community, and social distance promotes dehumanization. The problem of social distance, stereotyping, and dehumanization are dangerous all by themselves, but mixing them with the dynamic of power creates even more cause for concern.

POWER AND ABUSE

Power can be dangerous in the hands of human beings. Both secular and Christian thinkers acknowledge the evil tendencies inherent in humanity.[20] Human nature is inclined to evil, and power exposes this tendency quickly. As Frederick Douglass notably observed, the conduct of his seemingly benevolent slave owner grew more wicked as she wielded the dangerous power over him.[21] Similarly, the Stanford prison experiment illustrated how quickly power can affect the character of those who hold it. Seemingly peaceful and well-adjusted college students were selected to participate in a mock prison experiment as either a guard or a prisoner. The experiment quickly became contentious as the behaviors of participants changed dramatically. Nonviolent, middle-class college students transformed in terms of their disposition and conduct, so much so that some of the students selected to be guards engaged in abusive behavior.[22] The Stanford prison experiment offers a glimpse into the human proclivity to abuse power. But we really need look no further than human history itself, which is replete with examples of totalitarian states responsible for catastrophic tragedies and death.

The police possess significant power over others.[23] They can detain, arrest, and apply physical force to gain compliance, and possess the authority to exercise deadly force. Bearing in mind the proclivity for evil in humanity, police power should be a concern we all share. And given the potential for the police to dehumanize racial minorities, police power over minorities should be an even greater concern.

When power and the dehumanization of a people group are mixed, you have a perfect formula for abuse. What's worse is that once a people group is dehumanized, abuse may not even be understood as immoral. Philip Zimbardo explains,

> Dehumanization is the central construct in our understanding of "man's inhumanity to man." Dehumanization occurs whenever some human beings consider other human beings to be excluded from the moral order of being a human person. . . . Under such conditions, it becomes possible for normal, morally upright, and even usually idealistic people to perform acts of destructive cruelty.[24]

Dehumanization explains why police officers who have clear moral boundaries and guidelines in their personal lives can cross those lines when acting as officers.[25] Once a person of color is dehumanized, an officer may not feel morally restrained from engaging in abusive practices, up to and including police brutality.

FORMING OFFICERS IN POLICE CULTURE

Everyday practical experiences in a particular culture or organization are far more effective in shaping an individual than any formal classroom because real formation takes place at the grassroots level of experience, practice, and application. Immersion in cultural practices forms habits that develop into virtues or an internal compass pointing to what we genuinely value and love.[26] In simple terms, actions shape the heart, and the heart is primary to the head when it comes to formation.

Police culture, therefore, is powerfully formative because it operates at the doing and feeling level, whereas formal guidelines and classroom training operate primarily at the thinking level. It utilizes the most powerful means of shaping both identity and reality for officers, and no formal guideline has the power to usurp the values and practices that emerge.

A new officer is immersed in the culture as an embodied individual. They interact with police supervisors and other officers embedded in police culture, and they are molded through everyday experiences that become habits. These deeply meaningful practices are grounded in a *telos*, or desired end, embodied by police supervisors and other officers in the department. The leadership structure is not simply taught; it is felt through experience. The police supervisor interacts with the new officer as a representative of an embedded cultural ethos. Additionally, the new officer feels the tension between other officers and communities of color, experiencing the emotions and adrenaline when applying force—all of which is powerfully formative.

Furthermore, social distance and the us-them mentality are not abstract cognitive conceptions but are lived emotional realities. The officer does not observe impersonal lectures presenting cognitive concepts but feels police culture through relationships with supervisors, peers, and community via formative embodied experiences. All of this amounts to a terrifying reality: the hearts of officers are being formed in dangerous ways that will lead them to abusive practices. Police culture convinces officers to pursue abusive practices with complete justification.

Solutions to immoral police behavior tend to ignore an important aspect of our humanness—the formative power of the heart. Therefore, when police reformers have tried to change behavior with formal classroom training and updated policies, it should come as no surprise that they do not work, as they are aimed solely at the head. External measures alone cannot change the police. The culture is simply too effective in forming officers. True change in law enforcement will require transforming the culture first to make real and lasting change possible.

HOW WE REALLY DO IT ON THE STREET

When I attended the police academy, I was trained in the formal rules and guidelines. At the end of four months, I returned to the police department and read the training and policy manual. At that point, I thought I had an adequate idea of how policing worked or at least the general rules of the game.

Shortly thereafter, I was assigned to four different training officers, spending a month with each officer. I was told to forget everything I learned in the academy so I could be taught the way things really work on the street. One night, I was dispatched to a prisoner transfer, which meant meeting the arresting officer, taking custody of his prisoner, and then transporting the person to jail for booking and processing. When my training officer and I met the officer, we discovered the man he arrested was severely intoxicated. I opened the back door of the officer's police cruiser to move him to my cruiser, but he was handcuffed, passive, and clearly confused. I asked him several times to step out without him responding.

Based on my training at the academy, I thought it best to remain patient, professional, and give him time to comply before I tried to help him out. Both the officer and my training officer were watching, so I wanted to perform properly. Since the man had not responded to my requests, I tried to gently guide him out of the back seat. He offered no resistance, but his intoxication made it difficult for him to cooperate. At this point, the arresting officer muttered, "We don't have time for this." He moved me aside, ripped the man out of the back seat, dragged him to my cruiser, and forcibly stuffed him into the back seat before slamming the door. He looked at my training officer and said, "Rookies. He'll learn." He and my training officer had a good laugh before he drove off. I was humiliated. It felt like I had failed as an officer.

It was a lesson I'd never forget. This was not an egregious case of police brutality nor did the arresting officer have any kind of track record for abuse. What this event illustrated, however, was that dehumanizing treatment was normal, unquestioned, and preferred at the street level. That simple encounter communicated to me that the drunk man did not deserve humane treatment, patience and gentleness are weak, and good officers are aggressive in the exercise of force. It was my first clear lesson in social distance, dehumanization, and power abuse.

CHAPTER 3

TOXIC LEADERSHIP AND THE HIERARCHY OF POWER

CONTRIBUTING TO A DANGEROUS CULTURE

ONE NIGHT, A YEAR into my active-duty career, I was assigned to work with a veteran officer. Because of the strict hierarchy in law enforcement, there was no need to discuss who would be driving. The senior officer wins that job every time. I deferred to him, extending the respect warranted an officer with over ten years of experience. As we drove away from the station, a call came in that an officer had been shot. When a fellow officer is down, the police mentality shifts. Caution gets thrown to the wind to get to the scene as fast as possible. We exceeded speeds of ninety miles per hour, flying down city streets and through residential areas to reach the injured officer.

Upon arrival, we ran up to the residence and saw him lying on the ground, bleeding profusely from his abdomen. His partner, a clearly shaken rookie, informed us the wound resulted from a shotgun blast from a gunman who fled the scene.

Instantly, my partner took control. Gathering a brief description of the suspect, he directed the rookie officer to stay with his partner until the ambulance arrived, and he directed me to follow him in pursuit of the gunman. Gun drawn, I followed the senior officer through backyards in the dark. Every fence line, bush, and blind corner posed a threat, as the gunman was clearly willing and able to ambush an officer. Not long into our pursuit, additional officers arrived on scene, one of them a sergeant. We were now a five-man team, and without any deliberation or hesitation, my partner deferred to the sergeant, who took control and began giving direction.

We approached a privacy fence that bordered an apartment complex. One officer from our group climbed the fence, and when he reached the top, the gunman fired at him from ahead. Immediately, the sergeant provided direction and leadership. He ordered us to kick in the fence and crawl through the opening so that we would not be exposed to another shotgun blast. Once on the other side of the privacy fence, with the sergeant in complete control, our five-man team continued through the large apartment complex, tactically clearing areas in an effort to capture the gunman.

As our search continued, our numbers grew to the point that we split into several teams of officers. We eventually took cover on the side of a building in the apartment complex and were preparing to move to the next building. The move was particularly dangerous, as reaching the next building required us to pass through an area bordered by a line of heavy brush, a perfect spot for an ambush. No sooner had we begun to move than the sergeant ordered us to stop. There was movement in the brush.

About thirty seconds later, the gunman emerged from the heavy brush at the far side of our building with shotgun in hand. Had we not listened to the sergeant, we would have passed in front of the concealed gunman without protection. There were two other officers on the other side of the building, so we ran toward the gunman to assist. As the gunman approached, the officers yelled, "Drop the gun! Drop the gun!" Ignoring the commands, the man raised the shotgun as he continued to press forward. Before he could get the shotgun leveled to fire, the two officers discharged their weapons. The gunman collapsed onto the ground. We ran up to him as he was falling, and one of the officers kicked the man's shotgun away. I assisted in handcuffing his blood-soaked arm. We called for an ambulance; but it was too late. An artery in his neck was gushing blood at a rapid rate. There was no stopping the bleeding, and I felt his arm go limp. Before the reality of the situation had fully set in, it was clear that he was dead.

Incidents like these do not occur every day, but when they do there is no time for discussion, confusion, or hesitation. Had we not immediately heeded the sergeant's direction to stop before the wood line, our team would have walked directly in front of a concealed gunman, completely exposed and without cover. It could have cost us our lives. At all times throughout this quickly evolving situation, I understood who was in charge. When a ranking officer commands, you obey—period.

The hierarchy of authority is a mainstay in law enforcement, and it is critically necessary as it can be the difference between life or death. But police hierarchy has problems as well. It increases the potential for the abuse of power, and when abuse does occur, there's often little that can be done by the line officer. As a rookie officer, I learned this lesson early. I inadvertently upset my sergeant, and he assigned me to the booking room for two weeks. Not a word was spoken, but I received the message loud and clear. I have seen officers face reassignment, loss of their cruisers, shift changes, moving to offices that were formerly closets, and ordered to wear heavy dress uniforms in summer weather—all actions designed by police leaders to send a clear and unmistakable message: remember your place and who is in charge.[1]

As a result, there is often a deep divide between line officers and police leadership. I believe the distance and power that accompany police leaders promote the devaluing of officers and even the dehumanization of subordinates, a combination that accounts for the common power abuses between police leaders and line officers. We must ask how this environment impacts the attitudes and actions of line officers toward citizens. If the relationship between the leadership and officers is already detrimental, how might law enforcement leadership avoid abusive behaviors that can arise from the bureaucratic hierarchy? This chapter will explain the evolution of contemporary leadership before highlighting how the organizational structure of law enforcement, authority, and power has not developed in the same manner as other contemporary organizations. Additionally, we will see how the dangers of these developments are cultivating a toxic culture through leadership.

THE EVOLUTION OF LEADERSHIP

Modern thinking about leadership has changed significantly since the beginning of the twentieth century. From 1900 to 1930, the emphasis was on control and power. During the 1930s the focus shifted to leadership influence rather than domination. Leadership studies from the 1940s to the 1970s continued to evolve, prescribing leadership as a reciprocal process with an emphasis on persuasion over coercion. And the 1980s emerged as a significant decade for leadership, exploding with "scholarly and popular works on the nature of leadership, bringing the topic to the apex of the academic and public consciousness."[2] Leaders evolved from authoritarian directors to the more collegial guides preferred today.[3] As such, contemporary leadership focuses more on relationship, influence, power distribution, and collaboration.[4] This emphasis underscores two primary themes relevant to law enforcement: power and organizational structure.

POWER AND ORGANIZATIONAL STRUCTURE

Authority and power are related concepts. An organization can grant authority, but to exercise power truly, followers must be willing to accept direction.[5] Contemporary leadership emphasizes the acceptance of authority from below more than the positional authority granted from above.[6] Given the move away from heavy authoritarian leadership, a leader only has the power to lead effectively when it is granted by the people under their authority. To better illustrate this point, we must distinguish between positional and personal power.

Positional power is derived from the organization and includes a title or position that grants control over resources, information, punishments and rewards, and the work environment.[7] An important aspect of positional power is coercive power or "the power over subordinates . . . based on authority over punishments."[8] At one time, coercive power was acceptable and consistently utilized. Given the evolution of leadership, however, there has been a steady move away from the use of coercive power.[9] According to Peter Northouse, coercion is antithetical to leadership.[10] Gary Yukl and Nishant Uppal assert, "Effective leaders rely more on personal power than on position power."[11] In simple terms, heavy-handed leaders who govern through authoritative postures and intimidation are the antithesis of modern leadership.

Therefore, we should not be surprised that personal power has gained greater acceptance in contemporary leadership, as it "is derived from the desire of others to please a supervisor for whom they have strong feelings of affection, admiration, and loyalty."[12] Leaders gain personal power by cultivating trust through their expertise, which can reward them with considerable influence.

The shift in leadership to appreciate the leader-follower dynamic may partially explain why personal power is preferred over positional power. Barbara Kellerman posits that history illustrates a shift from top-down leadership to a more equitable distribution of power.[13] The trend over the last century has been toward organizational power sharing and leadership influence.[14] Top-down authoritarian leadership, which ignores the leader-follower relationship dynamic by relying on coercion, has been replaced by the relational modern leader who leads by influence.

With the emphasis on the power of influence and the rejection of coercive power in leadership, it is not surprising to find organizational structure has changed throughout the twentieth century as well. Generally speaking, there has been a move away from the strict formal structure with centralized power to a more informal structure where power is shared and teamwork is emphasized. Since the 1990s, organizations have adopted the trend of shifting from "hierarchical relations" to "collaborative relations" where "peer networks" replace "chains of command."[15] In other words, the changes in leadership power coincide with the softening of the hierarchy and the flattening of the organization, all of which create unique challenges for law enforcement.

LEADERSHIP AND ORGANIZATIONAL STRUCTURE IN LAW ENFORCEMENT

Despite the contemporary trend to soften the hierarchy and distribute power and authority throughout the organization, police departments are generally hierarchical, consisting of a strict top-down leadership scheme.[16] In fact, some argue that police departments become more hierarchical and bureaucratic over time.[17] Because of the strict hierarchy, power is centralized with the chief, who delegates power to lower levels.[18] Higher ranks have more authority than lower ranks, meaning the structure shapes the distribution of power and authority.[19]

This strict structure promotes social distance between ranks,[20] where police leaders view themselves as "far superior" to the officers they supervise.[21] This social distance can result in dehumanizing subordinates.[22] One reason for the social distance and tendency to dehumanize is that the same mentality that officers can have for the public exists in police leaders concerning the officers they oversee: the us-versus-them mentality.[23] The contentious relationships that form predicated on this mentality can result in abusive or toxic leadership practices such as coercion, intimidation, harassment, and unethical leadership behavior by police supervisors.[24]

Most concerning, the behavior of police leaders impacts the behavior of patrol officers along with their moral decision-making.[25] In fact, abusive leadership has been found to "undermine followers' moral courage."[26] Colwell and Huth posit that a police supervisor can be "viewed as a social terrorist spreading hostility and cynicism through the rank and file as well as the community they 'serve' like an epidemic."[27] Their description is eye-opening, alerting us to the real danger abusive leaders pose to their communities through their toxic influence on police officers.

The organizational structure and the centralized power in law enforcement create a landscape for leaders to become socially distant, dehumanize followers, and abuse power. This leadership model influences officers to reciprocate the same pattern of behavior toward citizens—toxic leaders forming toxic officers. The leadership, therefore, is helping to cultivate and maintain the tendency in police culture toward social distance, dehumanization, and abuse. Certainly, the strict structure in law enforcement can be a problem; however, the solution cannot be to formally soften the hierarchy or lessen the positional power that accompanies rank. As the opening of this chapter illustrated, the police are faced with dangerous and quickly evolving situations that demand a clear understanding of who is in charge and the duty of officers to obey orders.[28]

MAINTAINING THE HIERARCHY AND REFORMING LEADERSHIP

Despite the prevalence and acceptance of the strict hierarchy in law enforcement, some leaders are aware of the problems that accompany it; however, they are also aware of the resiliency and necessity of the structure. Therefore, they advocate for a pragmatic approach that addresses problems with the structure while not abandoning it.[29] So as we think about police reform and specifically how leadership can effect change, we must realize any leadership paradigm that requires abandoning the fundamental organizational structure in law enforcement is likely unrealistic. The evidence suggests the structure in law enforcement is here to stay. For a better leadership model to take root, it must operate within the current structure while both addressing and mitigating the problematic aspects.

Additionally, as we think about how police leadership and culture share the phenomenon of social distance, dehumanization, and power abuse, we may question, Did the culture groom the leadership or has leadership built the culture? There's no objective answer here, but what is certain is that leadership and culture interact in a cyclical fashion of influence where dehumanization and abuse are pathogenic—a trend among law enforcement we should all be deeply concerned about. What happens when a toxic officer must make a split-second decision on whether to exercise deadly force? What happens when an officer's trigger finger is controlled by a mind formed by a culture and leaders who do not promote the dignity and value of people, especially when it comes to racial minorities?

THE GOLDEN RULE OF POLICE LEADERSHIP

Treat others as you want to be treated. Universally, we recognize the golden rule as a beneficial guideline for behavior and ethical leadership. Yet, police leaders consider it an impediment to command and control. Though few would dare to say so, their actions prove their convictions through coercive and unethical practices in service of maintaining control. Thus, the golden rule in police leadership is *"Do unto others as needed for control."*

As a young officer, I was assigned to a three-person unit in a low-income housing development. The three of us got along well, but as I began working overtime in another unit, the senior officer politely suggested I desist, considering the practice a threat to our unit. I reckoned it was none of his business, so I ignored his request. Not long after, I arrived at work and received a letter from the captain informing me that I had been assigned new hours and new days off "effective immediately." My new schedule was crafted to be least favorable for my family, conflicting with specific activities we participated in regularly. The senior officer in my unit knew my preference when it came to schedule, activities, and the like, and while the letter explained the changes were predicated on "operational needs," I knew they were designed to teach me a lesson. The senior officer knew it. The captain knew it. And they both knew I knew it.

For weeks, I suffered the inconvenience with no end in sight. So I decided to violate an unwritten rule and lay my cards on the table. During a day shift where I was partnered with the senior officer, I told him I should have heeded his warning and I would not be working the overtime in the other unit any longer. I said, "I'm tapping out. Can I have my schedule back?" At first, he denied having any clue what I was talking about, but I pressed the issue, assuring him I was being genuine and harbored no hard feelings nor ulterior motives.

I will never forget how he looked at me in that moment, considering whether to take me at my word or continue the game. Then, without a word, he pulled out his cell phone, called the captain, and said, "These are his words: I'm tapping out." After a brief exchange, he hung up the phone and told me I would have my original schedule back the next day.

The senior officer did not dislike me, nor do I think he was trying to be vindictive. Rather, he did what he thought was necessary to maintain control of his unit. This golden rule of police leadership has flourished in a structure that promotes social distance, dehumanization, and abuse. Given this reality, what types of practices should we expect to surface among officers? In the next chapter, we will explore this question while taking a closer look at current strategies in law enforcement.

CHAPTER 4

BIAS AND BRUTALITY

THE FRUIT OF CULTURE AND ETHICS

IN THIS CHAPTER, we will consider how enforcement is the centerpiece of policing and how the prevalent strategies of law enforcement drive commitment to it in the unquestioned assumptions of officers. When I describe enforcement as the centerpiece, I mean that police tend to view it as the primary if not the sole means for solving problems, which allows them to enforce their way to grievous consequences, even with good intentions. Sadly, I know this to be true not only based on research, but through my own experience.

I was once assigned to a local high school as a resource officer. It had by far the largest population of African American students compared to the other high schools in the area. It was also where I received my education during the late 1980s and early 1990s. Embedded in an impoverished community, all extracurricular activities, including sports, were canceled at the end of my sophomore year due to financial problems. The crack epidemic was in full swing at the time, and our school was inundated with gang activity. Shootings, murders, and other violent crimes began to escalate in the area, and their effects were felt on campus. By my senior year, I witnessed teachers being attacked and students jumping one another. During one fight, the principal tried to intervene as a group of boys punched and kicked a fallen student only to have the attackers turn on him. One narrowly missed landing a punch to the principal's face, instead striking the door behind his head. Incidents like these would have been unthinkable just four years earlier.

Although sports eventually returned and the hardworking teachers and administrators did their best to mitigate the decline, I was not surprised by the condition of the school when I returned as a resource officer twelve years later. I did, however, underestimate just how far it had declined. My first month on the assignment was truly eye opening. During that time, I had to physically restrain five students, break up large fights, arrest drug dealers, and confiscate guns from students who brought them to school. Seemingly innocuous encounters, like asking a student why they weren't in class or escorting them with a hand on their back, could spark a profane tirade. I was baffled by this level of aggression, as I rarely encountered it during casual encounters in the streets.

The violence continued to escalate among students, and we had a particular problem with fights in the cafeteria. On one occasion, I came into the cafeteria and witnessed a young man I believed to be a student attacking another student. When the aggressor saw me approaching, he took off running. I chased him through the hallways and out the exit doors. We ran for a few blocks before I tackled him and secured him in handcuffs. I learned that he was not a student but an adult drug dealer who had come to collect a debt. In another incident, one student chased another student around the cafeteria with a survival knife that he'd brought from home.

I met with the principals to suggest a solution. I outlined a zero-tolerance approach where anyone caught fighting in the cafeteria would be charged with disorderly conduct, and if I could determine the primary aggressor, that individual would be charged with assault. They agreed to the approach and made an announcement to the students warning them of the new consequences they would face for fighting. I kept to the plan, charging every student I could, and in a relatively short period of time, the fights lessened. From my perspective, it was a success, and I had arrest statistics to prove it.

Then I had a conversation that radically altered my view. The local Marine recruiter, an African American man, informed me that every student I charged with assault would not be able to enter the military without a waiver. For many young adults in these kinds of communities, especially racial minorities, military service is a path to a brighter future, and I had barred the way for them. I had never considered the broader consequences of my zero-tolerance plan. Even though my heart was in the right place, I had engaged in what many would describe as disproportionate enforcement that bore fruit as a systemically racist practice that limited options for these kids by stamping them with a criminal record.

To this day, I am grieved over my actions. I acted in ignorance, but that doesn't excuse me from blame. Ironically, reflecting on my personal experience helped provide needed perspective for me. When I was a freshman, I initiated a fight in that same cafeteria and was never charged with a crime. After graduating, I served in the Army, and my experience in the military moved me to the top of the civil service police list, allowing me to begin my career as a policeman. Clearly, my life would have been radically different had I been treated the way I treated those students.

You might be wondering why I failed to see how destructive my actions would be on these students' futures, and the answer is the formative power of police culture. I was shaped by the officers around me as we interacted in real-life experiences on an everyday basis. Jaded, cynical, and emotionally indifferent attitudes garnered the greatest respect, and the officers who refused to tolerate any form of disrespect were treated as models to emulate. I was trained by an officer who fit this mold. He wore a leather jacket, looked angry all the time, and demanded nothing less than complete respect from the public. On one occasion, I thought I had handled a call for service correctly, but when I returned to the car, he yelled, cursed, and even threw a clipboard at me. In his assessment, I had used my authority inadequately and tolerated unacceptable behavior. Experiences like this are deeply formative.

The negative effects of my actions are obvious in hindsight, but my response to the problem at the time was automatic due to a police culture that promoted social distance and dehumanization. My unquestioned belief in the ethic of enforcement justified my actions. Police culture is blinding, and it's easy for officers to lose sight of people and only see problems. It has created an ethic that systemically racist strategies of law enforcement have been built upon—strategies that are organic to police culture and promote biased policing and brutality toward racial minorities, particularly African Americans. Like my zero-tolerance plan, officers adopt these practices without thought or reflection concerning the collateral damage and long-term implications.

THE EMBEDDED POLICE ETHIC—UTILITARIANISM

During my twenty-four years in law enforcement, I cannot recall a single conversation or shred of training material addressing moral philosophy, but the core ethic embedded in police culture bears out in a regular commitment to utilitarianism. Police ethicist Joycelyn M. Pollock defines it this way: "Utilitarianism holds that morality must be determined by the consequences of an action. Society and the survival and benefit of all are more important than the individual. Something is right when it benefits the continuance and good health of society."[1] Simply put, the end justifies the means. The utilitarian ethic in policing is an embedded presupposition unconsciously recognized and universally accepted. Cyndi Banks captures this reality in a description worth quoting in full:

> The [police] culture requires that police should never hesitate to use physical or deadly force against those who *deserve* it. Given that the role of police is to fight crime,

police culture views due process as a process that merely protects criminals and therefore as something that should be ignored when possible. From this perspective, rules concerning the protection of suspects and accused persons should be circumvented when possible, because the function of rules, so far as the police are concerned, is simply to handicap them in carrying out their true functions. Similarly, lying and deception are considered integral parts of the police function.[2]

Although most officers are probably unfamiliar with utilitarianism in a formal sense, they operate regularly under its influence. Consider the debate about stop and frisk and pretextual stops. Under the rule of stop and frisk, police are authorized to stop people who have not committed a crime if their conduct seems suspicious enough for the officer to believe "criminal activity is afoot."[3] If the officer has a reasonable suspicion, he or she can stop someone to frisk them for weapons. Additionally, an officer employs a pretextual stop if he or she observes a minor violation committed by someone they believe to be in possession of drugs or involved with other criminal activity beyond the minor violation. In this instance, the officer will stop the person for the minor violation with the intention to conduct a frisk or search and ultimately discover the drugs or other criminal offense. For police, these are essential and ethical practices for fighting crime because the end justifies the means. Jonathan Blanks, however, argues, "Pretextual stops are one part of a larger and deeply troubling mélange of legal fictions, intentional deception of the innocent, and perverse incentives that undermine the perceptions of legitimacy of law enforcement, particularly for black Americans."[4] Unfortunately, this kind of argument is rejected by a culture that has dehumanized a population and adopted a utilitarian ethic.

Police defend tactics like stop and frisk and pretextual stops by pointing to the drugs and weapons seized by using them, all the while ignoring the number of people who were stopped due to pretextual stops and frisked in their own neighborhoods and communities. They also ignore the feelings of those who have solid grounds for feeling mistreated and harassed. If officers were honest about how many innocent people they have stopped, it would be the overwhelming majority. They would also have to admit they are not really concerned how these innocents were inconvenienced and possibly harassed, or how minority communities at large feel. These are not considerations within a utilitarian ethic. Sadly, many Americans, Christian and otherwise, have ignored the voices of our minority brothers and sisters who have called for equal treatment. I wonder how silent we would remain if the police regularly implemented stop and frisk and pretextual stops on a college campus or in suburban America.[5]

The utilitarian ethic is deeply embedded and organic to police culture. It clearly contributes to the tension and violence between the police and communities of color. When a dangerous culture with an erroneous understanding of justice embraces a utilitarian ethic, one should not be surprised if a pattern of abuse emerges.

INTELLIGENCE-LED AND ZERO-TOLERANCE POLICING

Although community policing gained some footing in the 1990s, the twenty-first century saw policing strategies drift from community-based approaches toward strategic models that emphasize the use of intelligence. Intelligence-led policing involves gathering statistical data to identify "hot spots" plagued by crime and prolific criminal offenders.[6] The data is analyzed and used to structure how the department will utilize its resources and personnel to reduce crime. Although intelligence-led policing is presented as a tool for police officers to utilize, it is a philosophy of policing in the sense that it rests on and communicates a foundational principle: the primary purpose of the police is to reduce crime through objective analysis.[7] Although crime prevention is a purported facet of intelligence-led policing, unquestionably, the primary means to accomplish the mission of crime reduction will always be enforcement.

Since intelligence-led policing focuses on crime through statistical analysis rather than characterizing neighborhoods as communities of valued people, neighborhoods are reduced to statistical categories: hot spot or non–hot spot. Intelligence-led policing is dispassionate, impersonal, and myopically focused on crime without any real consideration of community, public approval, or the corollary effects of police action aside from its impact on crime. It is an attempt to objectify policing, and the effort to remove, or at least ignore, the subjective nature of people may also contribute to the dehumanization felt so poignantly by communities of color. The impersonal and dehumanizing tendency of intelligence-led policing makes it an attractive choice for a police culture prone to such characteristics. A dehumanizing culture with a dehumanizing police philosophy should be a cause for concern, but even more frightening is the combination that results in the method of enforcement predicated on intelligence-led policing, namely, zero-tolerance policing.

Zero-tolerance policing is a method of enforcement characterized by aggressive enforcement against all crime, even minor offenses like jaywalking, which are almost never enforced in neighborhoods that have not been categorized as hot spots.[8] This methodology focuses on surface-level enforcement and is not concerned with underlying social issues or relational concerns of the community.[9] Essentially, the police identify hot spots through intelligence-led policing and aggressively enforce all violations, no matter how minor.[10]

This is a particularly popular strategy in urban settings where large concentrations of African Americans and other people of color live. Minority neighborhoods become targets of this disparaging strategy, which is justified by the belief that enforcing petty and insignificant violations deters crime. In other words, enforce jaywalking and prevent murders. Stop and frisk everyone and we'll finally win that war on drugs. I'm only exaggerating slightly as the hyperbole exposes the flawed reasoning zero-tolerance policing is founded on.[11]

Given the inhumane nature of zero tolerance, we should not be surprised to learn the method "has captured the imagination of many in the police community, in part because it uses tactics quite familiar to the police."[12] It has gained traction by remaining consistent with the historical trend away from community and toward a focus on impersonal enforcement. Also, the cultural trend of social distance and dehumanization philosophically aligns with the intelligence-led/zero-tolerance enforcement, where officers enforce without discretion or relational considerations.[13] The police are simply enforcers separate from and above the community where this strategy is an organic expression of the leadership, ethic, and culture.

OPPRESSION AND SYSTEMIC RACISM

Writer and activist Michelle Alexander argues that the means of social control for African Americans has evolved throughout American history. Slavery was replaced by Jim Crow, and Jim Crow has been replaced by mass incarceration.[14] The mass incarceration of people of color has labeled many African Americans as felons, and as felons they are denied certain basic rights. Like slavery and Jim Crow, the legal system ultimately reduces African Americans to second-class citizens, or the "undercaste."[15]

According to Alexander, the police are instrumental in this process, and their practices are systemically racist and oppressive. She argues that police have the authorization and latitude to target African Americans through the so-called war on drugs that began in the 1980s—well before intelligence-led policing. In the 1980s, the police were authorized and encouraged to target African Americans in African American neighborhoods as a primary strategy in the war on drugs.[16] Alexander notes that the war on drugs could have been waged anywhere drugs were prevalent, like college campuses or suburbs, but "when the police go looking for drugs, they look in the hood," and "the hypersegregation of the black poor in ghetto communities has made the roundup easy."[17] In short, the 1980s and 1990s resulted in the police targeting African Americans concentrated in urban neighbors through aggressive enforcement,[18] leading law enforcement to engage in systemically racist and oppressive practices.

Although many in law enforcement disagree with Alexander, her argument should be concerning for the police. First, one could make the same critique of intelligence-led/zero-tolerance policing today. The police implement zero-tolerance enforcement in low-income urban communities comprising large populations of African Americans and other people of color. Jack Green, a police scholar writing from a pro-police perspective and who understands zero-tolerance policing as a legitimate practice, notes that zero-tolerance policing has "historic roots" in enforcing slave laws and drug laws, particularly in public housing.[19] Additionally, he describes zero-tolerance policing as a "blunt instrument" of "punitive and control-centered criminal justice culture" designed to send a message.[20] Even a pro-zero-tolerance policing perspective concludes this methodology has roots tracing back to slavery, reflects the dangerous police culture, and is aimed at African American communities. Even more than police strategies during the war on drugs, today's intelligence-led/zero-tolerance policing can result in exactly what Alexander describes: "The legal rules that structure the system guarantee discriminatory results. These legal rules ensure that the undercaste is overwhelmingly black and brown."[21]

A second, less arguable concern about intelligence-led/zero-tolerance policing is how it cultivates mistrust of the police in minority communities where people of color believe their neighborhoods are targeted.[22] At a minimum, this form of policing increases the tension and contributes to contentious encounters. In short, the current strategy in policing unfairly targets communities of color and exacerbates the mistrust and tension that can result in civil unrest.

THE NEW JIM CROW 2.0

I witnessed the war on drugs as a teenager, and many of my friends suffer the effects from it today. Marked as felons in their teen years, they have yet to recover even now in their late forties and early fifties. They were irrevocably impacted by laws that overwhelmingly targeted African Americans and other people of color.

As a rookie cop, we were still waging "the war on drugs," so I knew that good cops go to the hood and make dope busts. We didn't need statistics to identify these areas. We knew where they were. Sadly and ironically, the areas we targeted in the late nineties at my department were the same exact areas we later targeted through intelligence-led policing. Similarly, we didn't have a formal methodology of zero-tolerance policing when I began my policing career, but it is exactly the enforcement we used. If we made a traffic stop in the hood, the person received a ticket. There was a different threshold for discretion and mercy in the more middle-class areas than in the impoverished urban areas, which were predominantly Black and Brown. At the practical level, nothing has changed from the war on drugs to the strategies today.

If the war on drugs was the New Jim Crow, then intelligence-led/zero-tolerance is the New Jim Crow 2.0, targeting minority communities with greater sophistication. The only real change from the more informal strategies and general guidelines that characterized the war on drugs to today's intelligence-led/zero-tolerance strategy is plausible deniability. For example, when intelligence-led advocates are confronted with the biased results, they simply note, "Computer-based analysis . . . eliminates any bias that might be inherent in human-based decisions to target perpetrators and neighborhoods where crimes are predicted to appear."[23]

The police are better than ever at targeting people of color in urban neighborhoods and have an objective statistical justification to hide behind. I think it is fair to say the officer becomes an agent of a precise racist system. Their discretion is taken away, and their enforcement actions are targeted toward communities of color. Even an African American officer will become an instrument of systemic racist enforcement when operating under the auspices of police culture and this strategy.

In fact, given the influential power of the police culture, the utilitarian ethic, and the current strategy, the race of the officer is, perhaps, irrelevant—a reality that the tragic death of Tyre Nichols underscores. Certainly, African American officers are not immune to the culture, and it has been my experience that the culture may be even more influential for an officer of color. White officers are more or less automatically accepted by the police culture; however, Black officers must first show they are more blue than Black before they are accepted. In other words, they must epitomize the police culture to truly be part of it. Devon W. Carbado and L. Song Richardson support my observation:

> The pressures black police officers likely experience to fit into their departments potentially compound the problem. Some black officers may believe that their failure to share and display fellow officers' racial assumptions about African Americans will engender the perception that black officers are "soft" on crime and criminality and "hard" on racial affiliation and loyalty. That perception would create an incentive for black officers to "work their identities" to disconfirm assumptions that they will insufficiently identify with being "blue" and overly identify with being "black." Overpolicing other African Americans would be one way for black officers to perform that work.[24]

Over time, police culture can numb *any officer regardless of race* to the humanity of racial minorities, and African Americans in particular, leaving the officer apathetic, where no moral conviction is felt as he or she implements oppressive and even violent measures. Perhaps that is exactly what we witnessed in Memphis. Five African American officers infected by the dangerous nurturing of police culture, abusing an African American man. Police culture and ethic do not discriminate; they are equal opportunity moral degraders, and surely the intelligence-led/zero-tolerance strategy operates with frightening impersonal precision regardless of the race of the officer in the cruiser.

The officer simply becomes an agent of the system, targeting and enforcing with dispassionate precision. Alexander posits that racism morphs and embeds but continues. Certainly this is the case with the prevalent strategy in law enforcement. When coupled with the zero-tolerance methodology, the intelligence-led philosophy is innocuous to most, but it is clearly dangerous and unethical. The police culture, specifically the utilitarian ethic that dominates law enforcement, is an organic foundation for this unethical strategy.

Additionally, given police culture—social distance that leads to dehumanization—and the police ethic, one can certainly maintain that the intelligence that could be used for prevention and problem solving through a cooperative effort with the community will likely be used to facilitate a more enforcement-centric approach. The core of the police mission is enforcement, and many urban police departments are enforcement-centric: either predicated on less sophisticated strategies of enforcement or more sophisticated strategies. Either way, the deck is stacked.

HARASSMENT, DWB, AND BRUTALITY

Given the distrust and friction between racial minority communities and the police, is it any wonder so many feel the way they do concerning the police? Driving While Black (DWB) is a common theme among African Americans. Many feel they are pulled over, harassed, and targeted simply for being Black. Others—including many White Americans—believe this idea to be ridiculous. But given the prevalent police strategy, is it really?

Imagine two men who work at the same company. One is African American living in an urban neighborhood, and the other is White living in a suburban neighborhood. The two have a conversation, and the African American man explains that in his neighborhood, it's a virtual police light show. Officers are constantly pulling cars over, stopping pedestrians, and patting down people on street corners. He goes on to explain that when driving home, he has been pulled over numerous times near his residence: once for failing to signal a turn while pulling into his own driveway, two times for braking over a cross walk at a stop sign, and another time for snow covering his license plate tag. He asks if his White coworker has ever been stopped for such violations in his neighborhood. Of course, the White man says he hasn't. Later, the White man talks with his friend who is a police officer. He explains that his coworker feels he is being targeted by the police for being Black. The officer assures him, he has never stopped or targeted someone for being Black and that the department has several Black officers.

In this scenario—which likely takes place daily, in some form or another—the African American man rationally concludes that he is being targeted and harassed (DWB). The White man rationally concludes that is not the case, based on his experience. And the police officer answers honestly that he has never targeted anyone for their color. Yet the African American man has been targeted—by the system!

Intelligence-led/zero-tolerance and its less-sophisticated forms cite African American people and other racial minorities for infractions that are never enforced anywhere else. These experiences exacerbate an already strained relationship with the police, and the frequent, disproportionate, and insulting encounters with a frustrated and understandably angry demographic will result in greater conflicts. When these conflicts occur, a culture that promotes social distance and dehumanization will give rise to abuse and brutality—a sad reality underscored by the history of the police.

LOUISVILLE PD AND THE DEPARTMENT OF JUSTICE

The Department of Justice (DOJ) released the report of their investigation of the Louisville Metro Police Department (LMPD) on March 8, 2023. The report concluded the LMPD used excessive force and unlawful detainments that disproportionately affected African Americans. Concerning the stops, the DOJ observed specifically that,

> LMPD officers routinely violate these constitutional limits. Many of these violations involve pretextual traffic stops, which LMPD relies on heavily in its street enforcement activities. In a pretextual stop, an officer uses a minor violation, like a broken headlight, as grounds to stop someone in order to investigate unrelated suspected criminal activity. According to LMPD reports, officers use traffic stops to "target offenders in high crime neighborhoods" and "address crime in neighborhoods affected by violent crime." Officers told us that when they are not responding to calls for service, they engage in what they call "proactive policing," where they look for equipment or registration violations that might generate pretext for a stop.[25]

This observation by the DOJ seems to reflect the intelligence-led/zero-tolerance approach. In fact, according to the report, in 2012, the LMPD launched an initiative to target "hot spots" with "aggressive pretextual enforcement."[26] Clearly, this is a textbook application of the intelligence-led/ zero-tolerance strategy that will certainly communicate DWB. Therefore, we should not be surprised by the following example in the DOJ report:

> In one case, an officer stopped a Black man for a broken headlight. The officer told his partner that he smelled alcohol and wanted to run field sobriety tests for impaired driving and "make sure there's nothing else going on." He told the driver to get out of the car. Instead of checking for impaired driving, the officer carefully searched the driver and then each of the two passengers, methodically checking through their pants pockets and examining each object he encountered—a pack of gum, receipts, cash, lip balm, and Neosporin. As he searched one passenger, he said, "I know it's invasive man, but you never know, you know?" As the driver and passengers sat on the rear bumper, the officer told them to take off their shoes and inspected them.[27]

Ultimately, the DOJ report sustained that African Americans experienced widespread disproportionate and oppressive enforcement, disproportionate force applications, excessive force, and explicit racial slurs at the hands of the LMPD. The DOJ attributes these occurrences not only to concerning practices but also to problems in leadership. In light of police culture, ethics, leadership, and strategy, as concerning as the DOJ report is, shouldn't it be expected?

The DOJ investigated my department for excessive force in 2009.[28] At the time, we did not have a sufficient reporting system to track and record instances of force; thus, there was little for them to find. Nonetheless, the DOJ made recommendations, and we complied, resulting in significant changes to reporting procedures and policy. Ironically, it was around that same period that the lieutenants were sent to our first intelligence-led policing conference—coordinated and sponsored by none other than the DOJ! In 2005, the DOJ cooperatively produced and released "Intelligence-Led Policing: The New Intelligence Architecture" and began to "push aggressively for intelligence-led policing";[29] in 2009, the DOJ released "Navigating your Agency's Path to Intelligence-Led Policing," in which they explain,

Navigating Your Agency's Path to Intelligence-Led Policing (ILP) serves as an overview for implementing the ILP framework within a law enforcement agency. The ILP approach is a process for enhancing law enforcement agency effectiveness. It also provides an organizational approach to gather and use many sources of information and intelligence to make timely and targeted strategic, operational, and tactical decisions, thereby enhancing law enforcement effectiveness. This document provides information on how the ILP framework can support existing law enforcement policing strategies.[30]

To be fair, intelligence-led policing (ILP) could be used in coordination with community policing, and ILP literature by the DOJ is quick to point that out. I am also sure ILP advocates can find examples where ILP has been used to support some form of community-oriented policing. However, this is not the norm. The DOJ's support of ILP is much like the fireworks law in Ohio. Until recently, it was legal to buy fireworks in Ohio but illegal to use them. Fireworks outlets in Ohio would sell mass amounts of fireworks in the summer months and, of course, had disclaimers that pointed out the law that the fireworks were not to be used in Ohio. Some stores even required people to sign statements that affirmed they would not use the fireworks in Ohio. If these outlets were accused of indirectly supporting breaking the law on the Fourth of July, they could simply note the disclaimers and probably provide an example of someone who bought the fireworks and drove to Pennsylvania. However, on the night of the fourth, the fireworks display always commences. These fireworks outlets exist only because the vast majority of their patrons buy and use fireworks in Ohio. They are clearly aware of this yet hide behind their disclaimers and rare examples. So does the DOJ. They can surely point to their disclaimers that associate ILP with community-oriented policing, and even point to some examples of ILP supporting community policing; however, every day in urban communities the fireworks display commensurate as ILP is faithfully anchored to zero tolerance, and the stop and frisk and pretextual stops light up the sky. The evidence is overwhelming.

Clearly, the LMPD geared ILP toward enforcement; and although the LMPD has racial problems that extend beyond the intelligence-led/zero-tolerance strategy, the statistically based accusations of disproportionate enforcement by the DOJ would have been sustained even if the LMPD had unbiased enforcement robots in the police cruisers. The robots would still have been directed toward hot spots (African American neighborhoods) where they would have implemented zero-tolerance enforcement (pretextual stops, enforcement of misdemeanors that are not enforced anywhere else, and stop and frisk), which would have surely aggravated residents and led to more conflicts and incidents of force. In other words, even apart from the troubling police culture, ethic, and leadership, intelligence-led/zero-tolerance will facilitate systemically racist practices and results.

The LMPD could truthfully say that part of the problem is that they simply did what the DOJ prompted by implementing ILP. Despite the clear evidence of ILP in the report, why didn't the DOJ mention the strategy as part of the problem? Perhaps it has something to do with the federal funds associated with ILP.[31] However, we are moving beyond the scope of this book, so I leave that matter to others to investigate.

STRATEGIES IN CONFLICT

Just before my retirement from the police, I was sent to a meeting hosted by a community group to promote community policing. A few police chiefs attended or sent a representative from their department. The thoughtful host presented the group with several questions aimed at prompting the advancement of community policing in local police departments. We broke into several smaller groups, and each group was assigned a question.

My group was led by an African American woman in her early thirties. She was intelligent, organized, and thoughtful. I explained to her the fundamental differences between community policing and the prevalent strategy in policing. She quickly grasped the concepts. She realized community policing and intelligence-led/zero-tolerance policing could not both exist in one institution. They are diametrically opposed. How can you build community support and cooperation to solve problems collectively while simultaneously implementing a strategy that targets and infuriates racial minorities?

Our discussion, which we later relayed to the larger group, should have taken the air out of the room. I posited that any move toward community policing could not truly take place until departments reckoned with the apparent conflict. Community policing and intelligence-led/zero-tolerance policing cannot coexist. Unfortunately, this seemed to go over the heads of the listeners, and the moderator was forced to continue as if nothing had changed. But the rational conclusion to my assertion was that the recommendations made by the various groups, all of which assumed there were no substantial impediments to community policing, were impossibilities and a waste of time until fundamental and foundational changes were implemented.

PART 2

THE PATHWAY BACK
TO SERVANTHOOD
AND PEACE

CHAPTER 5

SERVANT LEADERSHIP AND FOLLOWERSHIP

FOUNDATIONS FOR POLICE LEADERSHIP

AS A NEW LIEUTENANT, I was full of optimism and excited to lead my people. I had new ideas that I was ready to devote time and energy to developing. Now that I was a peer with the other lieutenants, I came to know them as individuals and friends—and I was shocked by their apathy and pessimism. Looking back, I imagine my fellow lieutenants were thinking, *He'll learn. Let's see how he feels this time next year.*

All lieutenants were invited to a bimonthly meeting with the chief and captains, and I couldn't wait to discuss change and better ways to lead the department. In the meetings, the ranking leader would typically introduce an issue or problem and give some direction on what could be done. He would then invite feedback from the subordinate leaders. I was shocked that almost all the lieutenants said nothing or simply affirmed what the ranking leader had proposed. Foolishly, I assumed the invitation for suggestions was sincere, and I responded with genuine ideas. It wasn't long before I realized my suggestions were irksome and dismissed out of hand. The meetings were essentially a ruse to feign democratic leadership and maintain the autocracy. As time went on, mild irritation progressed into outright hostility toward my suggestions. Clearly, I was a slow learner.

Of course, the tension went beyond meetings. On one occasion my decision as the ranking officer at a call for service evoked an extremely aggressive response. A higher-ranking police leader learned of my decision, and although he was not at the scene of the incident and did not have all the facts, he wanted me to make entry into the residence. Once back at the police station, I tried explaining to him the facts at hand, clearly outlining why we didn't meet the criteria for a warrantless entry, which required consent or exigent circumstance. He immediately became irritated and continued arguing, all the while I tried to remind him of the undeniable objective facts— we had no warrant, no consent, and no affirmable emergency to make entry into the private residence. As the confrontation continued, I eventually became frustrated and said, "No warrant. No consent. No emergency. No entry. If you want to go in, you go out there and give the order." At that point, I saw the rage in his eyes. He raised his finger in my face and stepped toward me aggressively. I moved backward until my back was against the wall. His finger was less than an inch from my face, and the toes of our shoes were practically touching. In no uncertain terms—which would not be appropriate to repeat—I was relieved of duty and sent back to my office.

Although this is an extreme example, the authority, hostility, and potential for an aggressive response underlies every encounter with a superior. Some are simply more intense than others. Although most officers intuitively perceive this reality, I doubt many understand that occasional outbursts or aggressive encounters with a superior have little to do with the leader having a bad day. Rather, they are an organic consequence of the culture in law enforcement.

Given my immersion in police culture and the regularity of these encounters, how did I begin to see law enforcement leadership as fundamentally flawed? Shouldn't I have been blind as well to the deeper issues? Fortunately, at the time I was experiencing police leadership, I was witnessing a qualitatively different leadership in another sphere of my life—my pastor's small group. He was a devout Christian, a loving man, and a strong leader, instrumental in taking our church from a small congregation to a large, thriving, life-giving church. Many of the associate pastors he discipled advanced to be senior pastors and are now leading large and thriving churches. His strength and leadership ability were unmistakable. In my naivety and ignorance, I projected assumptions concerning leadership into him that I had seen modeled in police leaders.

But watching him, I quickly learned how wrong my assumptions were. I was shocked by his gentleness and how he balanced love with firmness when needed. He was nothing like the leaders I had encountered. I was amazed at how well he led the church and the unity and efficiency he inspired in his staff and support leaders. His example helped me to begin to see the deficiency in police leadership. While I saw him lead with humility and gentleness, I was simultaneously experiencing many police leaders exemplify hubris and dominance as the department delved deeper into disfunction, disunity, disorder, and subpar service.

This juxtaposition opened my eyes to the possibility of pastoral leadership in law enforcement, and when I began my doctoral studies years later, I discovered a secular leadership theory recognized by law enforcement that could provide the gateway for Christian leadership to be appropriated by police leadership.

SERVANT LEADERSHIP AS A STARTING POINT

Servant leadership, if incorporated into the current law enforcement structure, has the potential to mitigate the problems of social distance, dehumanization, and power abuse. It could also facilitate a shift toward contemporary leadership, thereby emphasizing leadership as a collaborative process of influence within the current law enforcement structure. However, servant leadership has serious flaws that must be corrected before it can be an effective model for the police.

The term *servant leadership* is an ancient concept, but its appearance in modern leadership literature can be traced to Robert Greenleaf, who wrote an essay on the topic in 1970 followed by a full-length book in 1977.[1] He believed the paradoxical roles of *servant* and *leader* could be united in an applicable model of leadership.[2] His conception of servant leadership dovetails with the move in contemporary leadership to reject autocratic, leader-centric models and embrace cooperative and collaborative models.[3]

Identifying a universally accepted definition of servant leadership, however, is difficult.[4] The concept is slippery, not easily reduced to a formula.[5] Nonetheless, its central ethos is that servant leaders are *"servants* who lead rather than *leaders* who serve."[6] And as servants, leaders stand with and not above their followers as a moral example focused on developing their people. Simply put, servant leaders seek to demonstrate the characteristics of servant leadership so they are reciprocated in followers. Rather than a rigid system of leadership, servant leadership centers on an uncompromising principle that is follower focused and applicable in multiple contexts.

Therefore, it is fair to conclude that servant leadership is primarily character focused, and the character of a servant leader can be expressed through specific characteristics and actions. Listening, empathy, healing, awareness, persuasion, conceptualization, foresight, stewardship, commitment to the growth of people, and building community are the core characteristics that communicate the "power and promise" of servant leadership.[7] As a servant, the leader is focused on the development of his or her people through these essential leadership characteristics and practices, directing them toward a shared organizational goal. Servant leadership embraces the paradox that focusing on people before the institution is how the organization will truly advance and flourish—for the people are the institution.

SERVANT LEADERSHIP AND LAW ENFORCEMENT

Servant leadership is a familiar leadership theory among police scholars and is promising for multiple reasons.[8] First, since it is character focused, it has the flexibility to be incorporated into the strict law enforcement structure. Its adoption does not require law enforcement agencies to abandon the formal structure that defines most police departments. Additionally, the general philosophy of a servant leader coupled with the ten servant leader characteristics previously listed provide a readily applicable guideline for servant leaders.[9]

Furthermore, servant leadership has the potential to mitigate problematic aspects of the organizational structure in police departments. Servant leaders are the "first among equals," not distant authoritarians,[10] and servant leaders are focused on serving their followers by listening, showing empathy, and furthering their development.[11] These qualities have the potential to combat the tendency among leaders to be socially distant and dehumanize their followers. They also combat the abuse of power. Greenleaf argued, "The trouble with coercive power is that it only strengthens resistance. And, if successful, its controlling effect lasts only as long as the force is strong. It is not organic. Only persuasion and the consequent voluntary acceptance are organic."[12] Servant leadership rejects coercive power, recognizing that influence is far more effective and long lasting.

Lastly, and most importantly, since servant leadership is intentional about forming followers into servant leaders, applying it to police leadership has the potential to develop these positive character traits among officers. This focus is so needed, especially when considering how toxic police leadership has groomed many officers for power abuse.

Not all police scholars consider the theory a perfect fit for law enforcement, however. Charles R. Swanson, Leonard Territo, and Robert W. Taylor note two potential obstacles. First, servant leaders can be perceived as weak.[13] Although law enforcement leaders should not behave like authoritarians, they often find themselves in situations where decisions are a matter of life and death. At times they must issue orders, and those orders must be obeyed. Law enforcement leaders cannot be perceived as weak. They must be obeyed, or the safety of officers and the public will be put at risk.

Second, servant leadership does not balance the needs of the organization with the needs of followers, particularly when there is a conflict of interest.[14] The police department, as an organization, must balance the needs of the community and the needs of the officers. Compromising to meet the needs of the officers can result in a disservice to the community. So balancing organizational needs as they relate to the needs of the community and the officers is important and complex.

In his analysis of servant leadership, Tim Cochrell identifies two additional concerning problems. First, the theory places too much trust in the basic goodness of human beings.[15] Given the power of officers, placing too much trust in an individual without strict accountability can be dangerous, even deadly. Second, servant leadership is constructed on a loose understanding of the world religions and lacks a solid philosophical foundation.[16] In today's society, a harmonious view of world religions is appealing and often accepted, but they do not have a synchronous conception of God, ultimate reality, the nature of humanity, human flourishing, or ethics. These foundational aspects powerfully shape not only how we understand the world and our vision for human flourishing but also how we live. This reality is most evident when worldviews are extremely disparate.

For instance, the apostle Paul and Friedrich Nietzsche had fundamentally different visions of the world, reality, and human flourishing based on their religious or theological understanding. Paul believed in a loving God who was active in a world infused with purpose and an eternal age to come. For Nietzsche, God was "dead" and there was only the meaningless world we see before our eyes.[17] Consequently, they had fundamentally different understandings of the ultimate end for life, the nature of humankind, reality, power, and the ethical use of power. For Paul, power entailed acknowledging dependency and surrendering to the will of God to pursue the greatest virtue of love.[18] For Nietzsche, power was an imperturbable will to conquer in an ultimately meaningless and temporal world. Whereas Paul admonished Christians to love their neighbor, Nietzsche demanded we drop our pretense and abandon love of neighbor and instead strive to be a "superman" who is no longer bound by a morality built on a futile hope of heaven.[19] Power defined by Nietzsche's philosophy and vision entailed morally unrestrained conquering. Power for Paul, defined by the Christian philosophy and vision, impelled service and love.

I have belabored this point because it is important that we understand the contemporary tendency to ignore how philosophy and vision predicated on differing religious or theological understanding significantly form our perceptions, conceptions, and actions. Without specific roots, the foundational ambiguity of servant leadership creates confusion related to the essential nature and categorical identification of a leadership characteristic, which will certainly guide a leader's ethical actions. Without a clear philosophical foundation informing its vision for flourishing, the characteristics of servant leadership can become nebulous, making application difficult if not conflicting.[20] Overcoming the weakness of servant leadership as a police leadership theory will require a firm philosophical foundation that can clarify the characteristics of a servant leader. It will also mean adjusting its practical application to maintain strength as a servant; balance organizational, follower, and community needs; and balance trust and accountability in officers.

CHRISTIAN LEADERSHIP IN LAW ENFORCEMENT

Christ-centered followership is a model of leadership designed primarily for pastors leading in the context of the church. Even so, it captures foundational truths concerning relationships, power, and mission that are also relevant to law enforcement, and when Christ-centered followership informs servant leadership, it can address the shortcomings of servant leadership in law enforcement.

Followership recognizes following as an important and indispensable part of leadership, emphasizing the cooperative relationship between leaders and followers. Additionally, followership and servant leadership share important commonalities in the relationship of following, leading, and serving. Christ-centered followership offers a unique lens for framing this relationship through a "distinctly Christian dynamic of leading as a fellow follower among people who are being led."[21]

To help explain Christ-centered followership, Michael S. Wilder and Timothy Paul Jones ask what if Jesus didn't lead like Jesus?[22] This question is designed to draw attention to the reality that some principles and modes of leadership have been inaccurately represented as Christian leadership.[23] In response, they utilize the Bible to construct a leadership model for pastors that is holistically Christian.[24]

In doing so, Wilder and Jones produce a concrete definition of leadership focused on the leader's identity and role in the community:

> The Christ-following leader—living as a bearer of God's image in union with Christ and his people—develops a diverse community of fellow laborers who are equipped and empowered to pursue shared goals that fulfill the creation mandate and the Great Commission in submission to the Word of God.[25]

Ultimately, Christ-centered followership defines leaders as "first and foremost followers" who are "inseparable from the community" and who use delegated power for a greater purpose than themselves.[26]

This definition underscores three important factors related to the leader's identity as a follower first: union, communion, and mission.[27] The leader lives in *union* with Christ[28] and in *communion* with God's people who are all made in God's image.[29] As a result, the power that accompanies leadership belongs to God and is to be exercised according to God's plan,[30] and the *mission* of the leader is grounded in God's truth, his purposes for creation, and the redemption of humankind.[31] Union, communion, and mission shape leaders into humble, community-grounded stewards who utilize delegated authority and power guided by God's truth and purpose.

Christ-centered followership also emphasizes an important leadership motif, namely the shepherd leader, but we will take that up in detail later. For now, we can sum up by noting that Christ-centered followership provides a core leadership principle that the Christian leader is a follower first, an ethos—union, communion, and mission—and the motif of a shepherd. These essentials provide the foundation for a synthesis with servant leadership to form a complete model of leadership specifically for police leaders.

THE GREATEST LEADERSHIP CHARACTERISTIC

After twenty-four years in law enforcement, I would be a fool to think I am exempt from the damaging effects of police leadership and culture. Although the opening of this chapter painted some leaders in law enforcement unfavorably, please don't think me innocent of similar behaviors. I have been brusque, condescending, and disrespectful. I have regrets about my conduct as a police leader, and even though I learned from many of my mistakes, it has taken time. Despite my shortcomings, I made a commitment early on to follow Christ first.

What did that mean? It meant I decided to conduct myself as a reflection of Christ and apologize when I failed. It meant leading admirably and asking for forgiveness from those I offended when I did not live up to that standard. I always tried to honor God with my commitment by modeling obedience and repentance.

I'm retired from policing now, and for a time I was a professor in a Bible college for incarcerated men. When I interviewed for the position, I met many of the students. One of them asked me, "What is the greatest leadership characteristic?" After my experience and immersion in Christ-centered followership, my answer was a reflex: "To follow Christ first."

Although I believe this is true, it is not exactly a precise answer to the question. Following Christ is the way to enter the perfect paradigm of leadership. So what is the greatest characteristic needed to follow Christ? Andrew Murray wrote,

> Men may have had times of great humbling and brokenness, but what a different thing this is from being clothed with humility, from having a humble spirit, from having that lowliness of mind in which each counts himself as the servant of others, and so shows forth the very mind which was also in Jesus Christ.[32]

Following Christ requires embracing one's inadequacy in humble dependence on him. Our pride makes this a painful recognition, which is why Murray notes how rare it is to find a leader worthy of being described as "clothed with humility."

What does it mean to be clothed with humility? This metaphor finds its meaning in the actions of Jesus, when the King of the universe donned a slave's garment, descended to his knees, and washed the feet of twelve dusty, dirty, first-century men. One of those men was Judas Iscariot, who Jesus knew would soon betray him. Could there be a more powerful depiction of humility than the Lord and Creator of all bowing to wash the feet of the "son of perdition," who would betray his Lord and master with a kiss, and deliver him to be scourged and crucified?

Humility is an essential attribute, a trait that cannot be compromised in police leadership where the structure inspires hubris and power abuse. For a leadership model to transform police culture, it must instill a new character and ethic in police leaders that inspires humility and servanthood. Bearing that in mind, we will turn our attention to seeing how Christ-centered followership can serve as a foundation for servant leadership in policing, helping police leaders embrace a new posture for a different kind of leadership.

CHAPTER 6

CREATING A NEW VISION FOR POLICE LEADERSHIP

THE SERVANT-SHEPHERD MODEL

I SPENT OVER TWELVE YEARS of my law enforcement career in leadership, and during that time I saw many officers rise through the ranks. One common observation was that when someone received a promotion, they changed—and not just in terms of their role, but in terms of their behavior. In police culture, the one in power is right and is not to be questioned. Officers take this posture with citizens too, which becomes evident anytime a citizen disagrees with an officer or challenges something they say. The officer will quickly change gears, politeness and courtesy dissolving into assertive authority, commands, and sometimes hostility. The underlying presupposition driving this kind of reaction is that might makes right. If this is the understanding and posture of an officer, what should we expect to happen when an officer is promoted to sergeant and has power and authority over their former peers?

I worked with an officer for years in the streets who was well-liked among his peers, so much so that when he was promoted, many officers were excited to have him as their sergeant. But it didn't take long for their opinions to change. Within a short period of time, he began reacting angrily anytime an officer disagreed with him. He would turn red-faced, take an aggressive posture, raise his voice, and point in the officer's face. Many were baffled by this change in their friend. But was it a change?

I don't believe so because that was exactly how he had responded to citizens when they questioned his authority. What the officers saw as change was consistency. He hadn't changed. Rather those who existed beneath his role in the police hierarchy had changed. He was no longer their peer, and superiors respond with hostility when challenged by their subordinates.

So how do we change leadership in a dangerous culture when the hierarchy cannot be compromised? Jesus said, "If anyone wants to be first, he must be last and servant of all" (Mark 9:35 CSB). In this simple statement, Jesus turns the police leadership model and ethic on its head. Law enforcement needs a model that can be incorporated into its organizational structure that can turn the typical police leadership and ethic on its head.

CONSTRUCTING A MODEL FOR POLICE LEADERSHIP

Although the model I am about to propose will be deeply grounded in Christianity, it is designed for universal application in law enforcement. John David Trentham's principle for the integration of the social sciences—inverse consistency—provides a protocol that can be adopted to create a Christian-based leadership specifically tailored for universal application in policing. The principle and protocol are a helpful guideline whereby Christ-centered followership and servant leadership can be integrated without compromising Christian authenticity or ignoring the contribution of servant leadership. Most importantly, the principle and protocol emphasize the context for leadership, thereby making the new model specifically suited for law enforcement.[1] The following steps were drafted based on Trentham's principle and protocol.

First, the core axiom of Christ-centered followership—that the leader is a follower first—and the ethos of union, communion, and mission will be formulated into four principles. These four principles will create a firm philosophical foundation that defines the nature of relationships, power, and mission for law enforcement leadership. Second, the shepherd motif will be used as a framework to categorize leadership action and relationship. Third, the foundational principles and the framework will define and clarify servant leader characteristics in law enforcement. Through these three steps, we will create a new leadership model for law enforcement that I will refer to as the servant-shepherd model.

The foundational principles of this model are just that: a foundation. A house is only as strong as its foundation. Similarly, a leadership model is only as strong as its foundation. Christ-centered followership is a leadership model grounded in a precise vision of the world that provides a clear picture for relationships, power, and mission for leadership. In other words, it has the solid foundation that can keep the house from crumbling. Therefore, it's imperative that we adopt the following four principles as the foundation for our new model.

Principle 1: Police leaders are followers first. Christ-centered followership defines leaders as "first and foremost followers."[2] This axiom is relevant for law enforcement. Ultimately, in a democracy, the people grant the police authority so that the peace of society can be maintained.[3] The will of the people is reflected in the laws that govern police authority and the mission of the police.[4] However, the dynamics of policing create situations that call for discretion. Therefore, laws alone are not sufficient, and ethical standards become essential to guide officers' decisions.[5] In other words, the police are subject to the will of the public articulated in the laws that govern the police and the ethical standards espoused by police agencies that reflect the spirit of enforcement.[6] Police leaders are public servants accountable to the public and held to a higher standard.[7]

Considering these guidelines, Edwin J. Delattre and Cornelius J. Behan posit, "Policing as a profession should take care to remember one other underlying assumption of constitutional government—the obligation of the governors to govern themselves."[8] This principle of self-governance is reflected in the reality that although the police enforce the law, they are first governed by the law and ethics that should shape enforcing the law. Certainly, the principle of self-governance is true and helpful, but it is best reshaped by the Christian principle of following first. Like pastors who surrender to a higher set of laws and ethics exemplified in Jesus, police leaders should not think in terms of self-governance, but endeavor to be followers first by humbly submitting to the laws that govern the police and the ethics articulated in department policies.[9]

Principle 2: Police leaders are one with the community of officers. The Christian concept of union helps us understand a leader's relationship to the community. The police leader, as a follower first, is united to a higher authority (laws and ethical standard) that places him or her in union with a people. The pastor is united to Christ and, therefore, is united to the church.[10] Likewise, the police leader is united to the laws and ethics that reflect the will of the people, which bond her to the community. As a result, the police leader is not above the community but a steward within it.[11] Similarly, the police leader is positioned among fellow officers—not above them.

The Christian ethic of equality of person is expressed in stewardship. For Christians, all people are made in the image of God and have equal value.[12] However, equality does not conflict with leadership position.[13] Essentially, stewardship is predicated on equality of personhood within rank structures. Therefore, law enforcement leaders are stewards among their people united to a higher authority and to their intrinsically valuable officers.

Principle 3: Authority and power should be used judiciously and benevolently. Unity leads to community. The police leader is in communion with their officers, and they share common goals related to their mission. The leader is responsible for developing and empowering officers to "pursue shared goals."[14]

Consequently, there are three implications concerning power. First, power is not intrinsic to the leader but delegated to the police leader from the community.[15] Second, power is shaped by the shared goals of the community of police officers not by personal agendas.[16] Third, power is to be shared so officers are equipped to achieve collective objectives.[17] The Christian concept of communion helps provide an accurate understanding of power for police leadership. Power is not intrinsic for personal use, but delegated, shared, and utilized for equipping officers for goals that relate to a higher purpose.

Principle 4: The primary mission is justice and peace. The Christian principle of mission provides a foundation to understand the mission of the police. For Christians, the creation mandate and the Great Commission largely define the concept of mission. The creation mandate calls for "cultivation" and "stewardship" of the world.[18] The Great Commission is predicated on the truth that the world is systemically flawed due to sin, and God will ultimately restore the world but is actively using people who proclaim the gospel in the present.[19] The creation mandate and the Great Commission can also clarify mission principles for law enforcement. First, although injustice is a reality of this fallen world, the Christian worldview affirms humankind's responsibility to bring order and justice.[20] Second, the Christian vision calls for humanity to participate in God's mission to restore peace. Consequently, the Christian foundation for justice and peace provides law enforcement with a helpful grounding philosophy to support the principle that *the primary mission of the police is justice and peace.*

Furthermore, the mission of justice and peace reflects the foundation of modern policing. Sir Robert Peel's principles were grounded in a single foundational maxim: "To keep the peace by peaceful means."[21] Peel asserted in his first principle, "The basic mission for which the police exist is to prevent crime and disorder as an alternative to the repression of crime and disorder by military force and severity of legal punishment."[22] This principle affirms justice as the primary mission of the police in two ways. First, the police are to combat disorder and crime, both of which contribute to injustice. Second, the police are to do so primarily by prevention and not by repression because enforcement has the proclivity for injustice.[23] Therefore, Peel understood—and the history of law enforcement illustrates—that enforcement can lead to injustice. Mission, as defined in Christ-centered followership, provides a solid philosophical foundation to support peace and justice as the mission of law enforcement leaders to implement in police departments.

THE SHEPHERD FRAMEWORK

Now that we have set the foundation firmly in place, it is time to frame our house. This section will use the shepherd motif to frame our leadership model by demonstrating how it can shape the general actions of a police leader and define their relationship with their followers. The Bible presents Jesus Christ as the perfect shepherd leader, a relational, caring, and personal leader who guided and protected his followers. The characteristics of a shepherd make the metaphor promising for police leadership as well as a much-needed construct to reform toxic leadership.

Shepherd function—the actions of the shepherd. There are three essential functions of the shepherd leader. Jones explains, "God refers to his people as sheep and to their leaders as shepherds—a metaphor that places leaders among the people, personally sustaining and safeguarding the flock."[24] *Therefore, the shepherd leader is (1) present, (2) protecting, and (3) providing.*

First, shepherd leaders are *present* with their officers. They cannot be distant but must lead from within. Second, the shepherd leader *protects* by safeguarding their officers and rescuing those who are in danger.[25] This does not imply that shepherd leaders compromise ethics to protect officers from wrongful actions. The police leader is not only a protector of officers, but also a protector of the community. Like pastors, police leaders must balance the function of protector in a varied context. Pastors must balance the role of protector in relation to the people of the church and the people of their community that are not Christians. Police leaders must balance the needs of their officers and of the people of the community. Rather than abandoning discipline, shepherd police leaders humbly institute discipline as a necessary function to protect officers and the community for the pursuit of peace and goodness for all.

Third, shepherd leaders *provide* for their officers. The function of provider includes practices outside traditional law enforcement leadership by focusing on provisions that will improve the lives of officers and promote peace. There are virtually no limits to this function, for the shepherd leader—who is one with the people—is motivated by compassion for their officers.[26] Police officers face stress, pressure, and danger in fulfilling their duty, and like all people, police officers struggle with family and personal issues. Police leaders can buy lunch for an officer struggling financially because of a divorce or go out of their way to facilitate a much-needed vacation day for an officer. The point is not to offer a list of responses but to simply point out that police leaders should be aware of everyday opportunities and respond with provision.

This shepherd leader stands in contrast to the distant or toxic leader in law enforcement. Jones notes, "The more time pastors spend with their flock, the better they will understand how people view the world, [and] in what areas they struggle most."[27] When officers know the leader is genuinely concerned and cares for their welfare because they have experienced their acts of provision—which sometimes require self-sacrifice—discipline is unlikely to be viewed as tyrannical. Instead, provision provides a foundation for discipline to be understood as protection. The shepherd leader is present, protecting, and providing. These three functions provide the functional framework of shepherd leadership to be brought together with servant leadership characteristics.

Shepherd connection—the relationship of the shepherd. Wilder notes, "Pastors are brothers with the members of their congregations, called to cultivate the identities of their brothers and sisters in Christ as redeemed sojourners, living stones, and suffering servants."[28] In the same way, police leaders, as shepherds, are *brothers and sisters* with their officers. A leadership role does not de-emphasize the familial relationship between police leaders and officers. They are all brothers and sisters among one family.[29] Consequently, police leaders should always emphasize this relationship with humility, remembering they are not "detached from or above" their officers, "but a family member within the community."[30] Police shepherd leaders value relationships over titles.

Second, police shepherd leaders are *fellow sojourners.*[31] Although the history of law enforcement illustrates the problems of the past, the police have made some helpful changes and reforms. The police leader, as a fellow sojourner, recognizes the past, emphasizes the positive changes, and acknowledges the police still have not arrived. Officers can disconnect themselves from the past or they can define themselves by the past. Neither approach is helpful. As fellow sojourners, police leaders can share in and help officers emphasize the reforms in law enforcement and the hope for the future without forgetting the past. Simply put, as sojourners, the officers and police leader share a journey of difficulty and hope.

Third, police shepherd leaders are *living stones.* This metaphor emphasizes the important role every officer plays as part of an organization sharing in the responsibility to fulfill an essential purpose.[32] The officers and the leaders are all valuable components of the police department and share the mission. In short, as stones in a shared structure, officers and police leaders are equally valuable in a shared mission.

Fourth, police shepherd leaders are *suffering servants.*[33] Law enforcement is an inherently dangerous occupation. Officers can suffer physical and psychological damage as well as hostility from the community, which makes suffering a real part of policing.[34] Officers and police leaders are fellow suffering servants.

SERVANT LEADER CHARACTERISTICS

Our house now has a firm foundation and beautiful framing. So, it's time to hang the drywall and fill in our walls. Just as a house's foundation and frame give the drywall support and a meaningful purpose, our leadership foundation and framework provide support and clarified meaning to the characteristics of servant leadership. The four principles (foundation) and the shepherd actions and relationship (framework) provide the infrastructure for the servant leader characteristics.

Present with the officers—listening, empathizing, aware, building community. These characteristics are critical pieces of the presence function of shepherd leadership. The servant-shepherd leader is a follower first and one with their community of officers. Therefore, they are not distant but humbly present, accessible, and concerned, spending time with their officers to better understand them.[35] Consequently, leaders are intentional about listening. Larry Spears notes, "The servant-leader seeks to identify the will of the group and helps to clarify that will."[36] Similarly, the servant-shepherd leader listens to understand and shape the will of officers, not according to their own desires but according to the mission of justice and peace.

Additionally, the servant-shepherd leader empathizes with officers. Spears notes that servant leaders are "empathetic listeners."[37] Informed by Christ-centered followership, the reason for empathy is clear, as a fellow brother or sister, the leader shares in a journey that involves suffering. The leader and the officers are a community united in one mission and, thus, share the experience, allowing for the leader to truly empathize.

Spears also states that servant leaders are self-aware and confront followers with disturbing and awakening realities.[38] Bonded by their shared struggle, their connection with officers has meaning and softens confrontations. They are present in the struggle, not distant overlords separated from the difficult realities of the law enforcement context. Furthermore, Spears explains, "This awareness causes the servant-leader to seek to identify some means for building community among those who work within a given institution."[39] The shepherd leader model guides this process, offering not only the means but also the ends for building community. The leader's relationship as a shepherd and the shared mission of peace become both the means and the end for building community.

Protecting—persuading, conceptualizing, foreseeing. Persuasion, conceptualizing, and foresight are servant leadership characteristics best applied through the protection function of shepherd leadership. The servant-shepherd leader desires to protect their officers from harm, endeavoring to influence and guide officers in the appropriate direction. For the servant-shepherd leader, power is given to be used judiciously and benevolently. They conceive of future problems and offer solutions to protect fellow officers from avoidable impediments in their shared journey. Servant-shepherd leaders are intentional about conceptualizing and foreseeing these problems that could impede not only the mission of peace but their officer's personal growth as well.

Providing—stewarding, healing, cultivating growth. Stewardship, healing, and commitment to growth are servant leadership characteristics best applied through the providing function of shepherd leadership. Stewardship underscores a posture that promotes provision. Servant-shepherd leaders are trustworthy, committed to their family of officers and the mission of peace and justice. Servant-shepherd leaders also have the opportunity to help officers heal from the tensions and difficulties they have experienced. Additionally, they understand that healing can transform officers, empowering them to engage more effectively in the mission of peace and justice.

Lastly, through faithful stewardship and promoting healing servant leaders are committed to the growth of their people. The servant-shepherd leader models a leadership style that is intentionally influencing and shaping officers to engage effectively in the mission of justice and peace.

OVERCOMING SERVANT LEADERSHIP SHORTCOMINGS

Now that our house is in place, let's review how we have overcome the weaknesses in servant leadership specifically related to police leadership. The servant-shepherd model moves beyond these weaknesses in at least four ways. First, unlike servant leadership, the servant-shepherd model is not founded on an ambiguous worldview. Rather it is firmly rooted in the Christian worldview, providing clarity to the otherwise nebulous servant leadership characteristics.

Second, servant leadership can be overly focused on the follower, making it difficult to apply when the needs of the individual conflict with the needs of the organization and community. The servant-shepherd model, however, provides clarity regarding purpose and relationship. Although there are

CHRIST-CENTERED FOLLOWERSHIP PRINCIPLES

1 Follower first   **2** One with community of officers
3 Judicious and benevolent use of power   **4** Mission of peace and justice

DEFINING
SERVANT LEADERSHIP CHARACTERISTICS

SHEPHERD FRAMEWORK

FUNCTION

Present
- Listening
- Empathy
- Awareness
- Building community

Protecting
- Persuasion
- Conceptualization
- Foresight

Providing
- Healing
- Stewardship
- Commitment to growth

CONNECTION

- Brother
- Redeemed sojourners
- Living stones
- Suffering servants

LEADER IDENTITY

INFLUENCING   SHAPING

OFFICERS

Figure 6.1. Servant-shepherd leadership model

distinctions among leaders, followers, and the organization, the united mission, relational unity, and protection function that incorporates discipline allow the servant leader to balance the context. In other words, the distinctions are recognized, but leadership decisions are based on the unity of the leaders, followers, and the organization as one people sharing in the same mission

Third, servant leaders can appear weak, but the servant-shepherd model emphasizes protection and discipline. Leaders in this framework avoid the appearance of weakness and are empowered to make difficult decisions involving discipline for the good of their people.

Lastly, servant leaders can be too trusting of followers and fail to provide accountability. The servant-shepherd model recognizes the value of people as well as the proclivity for unethical behavior. Therefore, the shepherd framework emphasizes presence and protection, recognizing officers need accountability for protection. Servant-shepherd leaders intentionally shape officers into servants and shepherds that do not engage in abusive practices. They provide accountability for the human proclivity to abuse power by shaping and empowering officers to pursue the mission of justice and peace.

PEACE AND TURKEY

During the latter years of my career, I supervised a three-person community policing initiative in a housing project in one of the worst areas of our city. As a patrol commander, I tried to model a gentle and respectful approach to any and every citizen—most importantly to people hostile to the police. I expected my officers to do the same. As a result, although I believe most of the officers appreciated me as a person, they believed my style of policing to be overly accommodating to the public. The new community policing unit—at least to many of the officers—was simply a platform for catering to the public and not real police work. The officers referred to the initiative as the "hug a thug" unit.

Although we were a community-friendly unit, we still had to maintain order. On one occasion, an African American woman in her twenties had allowed her boyfriend to live with her, and he was dealing drugs. Undoubtedly, he was a nuisance, and we had a duty to address the problem. The young woman—let's call her Sandra—was confrontational, rude, and clearly supportive of the criminal activity taking place around her apartment. Given the problem, I knocked on her door one afternoon to deal with it. I was abrupt with Sandra and let her know we would arrest her boyfriend and have her evicted. She of course responded with anger, taking my comments as a threat. Eventually, we arrested her boyfriend and barred him from the property. She was never evicted as she was not connected to the events relating to her boyfriend's arrest, but she did become bitter toward the unit, and probably toward me specifically.

A few months later Thanksgiving season arrived, and our unit received several turkeys to distribute to the residents of the housing unit. Immediately, I began to think of residents that we liked and appreciated who should receive the turkeys. A young officer in the unit who was a devout Christian had a different approach. He suggested we give the first turkey to

Sandra. I agreed, and we did exactly that. The young officer knocked on her door, and when Sandra answered, she cursed at him and asked what he wanted. The young officer let her know that he had a turkey for her, and that he wanted her and her children to have a happy Thanksgiving. Her countenance immediately changed, and she began to cry. She graciously took the turkey offering thanks. The tension between us and her disappeared, and we had peace.

I don't tell this story to suggest that unexpected gifts would resolve the tension between communities of color and the police, but it shows that more than just a leadership model is needed to combat the police culture. Even though I was countercultural and intentional about being an example for officers, when I was faced with a real problem, I reverted to a utilitarian ethic and suspended my respectful, gentle, and peaceful posture for abruptness and enforcement threats. Certainly, we were right in investigating and arresting Sandra's boyfriend, but I did not need to suspend my posture of peace to treat her with disrespect. I lost my focus on peace, and the young officer clearly knew it. His heart was oriented toward peace whereas mine had reverted to conflict.

The police need more than just the servant-shepherd leadership model to combat the subtle influence of police culture. We need an ethic firmly buttressed to the leadership model so that our actions are concretely oriented toward peace in our communities. In the next chapter, we will consider the moral compass that keeps the servant-shepherd leader's heart fixed on peace.

CHAPTER 7

FINDING TRUE NORTH

THE MORAL COMPASS LEADING TO PEACE

AS IMPERFECT PEOPLE, we have a skewed moral compass. Like an actual compass, our moral inclinations may be generally oriented toward righteousness (magnetic north), but they remain slightly off course from perfect righteousness (geographical north or true north). And like a person using an imprecise compass, we will eventually find ourselves grossly misguided. To accurately navigate the moral landscape, we need to be adjusted so the intentions of our hearts point to the true north of righteous action.

Given the power entrusted to police officers, precision becomes most crucial, especially in volatile circumstances where their moral decisions can be a matter of life or death. Police need a recalibrated moral compass aimed at the true north of peace—a clear and virtuous ethic that provides direction through the jungle of cultural moral distortion.

I believe the Christian faith offers this ethic. Paul wrote to Christians during a time of inner group conflict, social injustice, and persecution when the temptation to abandon one's moral guiding principles was ever present. He urged them not to be "conformed to this age, but be transformed by the renewing of your mind, so that you may discern what is the good, pleasing, and perfect will of God" (Romans 12:2 CSB). John Stott contrasts the value system of the first-century Roman world with the Christianity alluded to in this verse, saying, "These two value systems are incompatible, even in direct collision with one another. . . . The two sets of standards diverge so completely that there is no possibility of compromise."[1] Christians had to hold fast to a new value system in a culture that emphasized a completely different ethic while immersed in a world that provoked responses grounded in an immoral ethic. Similarly, police officers need not be conformed to the police culture but need to have their minds renewed by a new guiding ethic—a countercultural moral compass.

Paul laid out the implications of this renewed mind in the turbulent first-century world:

> Let love be genuine. Abhor what is evil; hold fast to what is good. Love one another with brotherly affection. Outdo one another in showing honor. Do not be slothful in zeal, be fervent in spirit, serve the Lord. Rejoice in hope, be patient in tribulation, be constant in prayer. Contribute to the needs of the saints and seek to show hospitality.
>
> Bless those who persecute you; bless and do not curse them. Rejoice with those who rejoice, weep with those

who weep. Live in harmony with one another. Do not be haughty, but associate with the lowly. Never be wise in your own sight. Repay no one evil for evil, but give thought to do what is honorable in the sight of all. If possible, so far as it depends on you, live peaceably with all. Beloved, never avenge yourselves. (Romans 12:9-19)

The practical implications were shockingly countercultural. Much like in Paul's time, the police need a countercultural ethic to guide them, and Paul's words here provide an understanding of how the Christian faith can fill that need. A new police ethic must depart from the old value system and serve as a moral compass that can combat the internal ethical formation of police culture and the difficult and provoking environment in which the police operate. Of course, this ethic must be appropriate and applicable for a secular police department. In this chapter, we will develop an ethical model that can deliver all the above.

LEADING CHANGE AS AN ETHICAL EXAMPLE

Given the embedded and obstinate nature of the police culture, the servant-shepherd leader needs a guiding ethical principle to strengthen their influence. Leading by example requires leading as an ethical example, and the change needed to guide police culture away from the dangerous tendency of social distance, dehumanization, and abuse must be grounded in a clear and unmistakable ethic.

Police brutality is unquestionably an ethical issue underscored by recent events of abuse. The death of George Floyd had a national and even global impact. Incidents of civil unrest erupted across the United States along with many peaceful demonstrations against racial injustice and police brutality. For some, the incident may have appeared as an isolated occurrence of police brutality, but for others—particularly African Americans—it was an event deeply rooted in a long history of injustice against African Americans, exacerbating a grief and anger spanning generations.[2] Seeing the video of Floyd's death inevitably compels moral reflection, as the officer's inhumane application of force and his seeming indifference is truly shocking.[3] Compounding the matter, before many could truly reckon with George Floyd's death, communities were confronted with the disturbing recordings that detailed Tyre Nichols's death. These incidents, along with the sad history of police brutality in America, underscore the importance of moral theory in policing. Certainly, in the wake of George Floyd and Tyre Nichols, ethical adjustment is necessary.

Christian ethics by nature compel a response. Stanley J. Grenz explains, "Jesus' ethic does not end with God's family. Instead, it leads to a widened concern. Disciples are committed to God's task of reconciliation. Just as they have experienced peace through receiving God's unmerited favor, so they should desire to become peacemakers."[4] From a Christian perspective, police officers are called to be peacemakers, and reconciliation is needed between the police and communities of color. Ethical change in policing is overdue, and the Christian ethic naturally emphasizes the peace and reconciliation that are clearly needed.

DEONTOLOGICAL ETHICS: RIGHT IS RIGHT ALL BY ITSELF

As we discussed previously, a utilitarian ethic lies at the heart of police culture, justifying an ends-justifies-the-means approach to policing. Deontological ethics, however, do not consider the result as the primary assessment of a moral action. Instead, the focus is on "right and wrong moral actions and moral laws and holds that some moral acts and rules are intrinsically right or wrong irrespective of the consequences produced by doing those acts or following those rules."[5] In other words, actions are good or bad based on the action themselves rather than their respective outcomes. Additionally, because of the emphasis on the moral nature of an action, deontological ethics emphasize the centrality of moral duty. This emphasis on intrinsic right and wrong and duty is important when the tactics of the police are being questioned and mistrust continues to grow, especially among African Americans.[6]

Immanuel Kant is perhaps the most notable deontological ethicist.[7] He called for a categorical imperative or an unconditional rule of conduct.[8] "Ultimately the categorical imperative states 'do your duty.' Hence in each situation we merely determine what our duty is and do it,"[9] and our duty must be determined by a universal principal or unconditional rule that can govern all actions. Many have criticized Kant for his attempt to capture a maxim for moral duty that supersedes all others in every situation. Considering this justified criticism, I will not propose an absolute maxim of duty but will instead introduce a central moral duty for law enforcement—that is right in and of itself regardless of consequences—that all other moral actions fall under and are generally guided by in the police context.

FINDING THE CENTRAL MORAL DUTY: PEEL'S EMPHASIS ON PEACE

As we noted earlier, Robert Peel's principles reflected one foundational maxim: "To keep the peace by peaceful means."[10] This duty provides a solid starting point for a core ethic in law enforcement, and it coincides with the Christian faith. Christian ethicist Stanley Grenz writes, "Just as [Christians] have experienced peace through receiving God's unmerited favor, so they should desire to become peacemakers."[11] Peel's maxim, however, seems to have been written in an overly optimistic form. Some actions of the police will never be considered peaceful, such as the need for deadly force to prevent a gunman intent on mass murder. To better apply this principle to reality, the core ethic of law enforcement would be better stated as, "To keep the peace through the most peaceably feasible means." Prudent peacekeeping is the heart of the officer's duty and the centerpiece for this ethic.

There are three essential Christian concepts that can enhance our understanding within the police context. First is the doctrine of the *imago Dei*, which teaches that all people are made in the image of God, a reality that has far-reaching implications for law enforcement. Wayne Grudem explains, "Every single human being, no matter how much the image of God is marred by sin, or illness, or weakness or age, or any other disability, still has the status of being in God's image and therefore must be treated with the dignity and respect that is due to God's image-bearer."[12] People's conduct or other outward identifiers, like race, are irrelevant with respect to the dignity everyone deserves. All people have intrinsic value.

Grudem warns of the implications if this reality is ignored: "If we ever deny our unique status in creation as God's only image-bearers, we will soon begin to depreciate the value of human life."[13] The *imago Dei* is an essential understanding that cannot be compromised. When people are dehumanized, the consequences are catastrophic. History is replete with examples of the dangerous combination of power and dehumanization, such as the subjugation of African Americans during colonial slavery or the attempt to exterminate the Jewish people in Nazi Germany. Given the us-them mentality in police culture and the tendency toward social distance and dehumanization, the reality of the *imago Dei* stands in firm opposition, demanding dignity and respect for every human being. Therefore, it must inform the duty of peacekeeping.

Reconciliation is also an important tenet of Christianity, affirming that sinful humans can be reconciled to the Father through Jesus Christ. This doctrine, however, does not only concern God and humanity but also has implications related to human relationships. "Humanity is reconciled to humanity."[14] Given the tension, mistrust, and violent encounters between police and racial minorities, reconciliation is vital to the duty of peacekeeping. The tendency toward social distance, dehumanization, and abuse makes reconciliation essential to this mission. The police need this change of attitude for unity to be restored.

Lastly, meekness is a crucial characteristic of Christian faith, but one that is often mischaracterized and misunderstood. The Greek word *praotēs* (or *praupathia* in the Greek of 1 Timothy 6:11) does not imply weakness or timidity. The apostle Paul implored Timothy to embrace this virtue, followed immediately by the charge to "fight the good fight of the faith" (1 Timothy 6:12). Paul's direction, therefore, is given in the context of leadership, toughness, and endurance. Andreas J. Kostenberger explains, "Paul wants Timothy not to be soft or timid but realistic and tough-minded."[15] W. E. Vine further notes that meekness comes from a position of power and "describes a condition of the mind and heart" that is the "opposite of self-assertiveness and self-interest," concerning service particularly in "dealings with the ignorant and erring" people.[16] Therefore, meekness relates to a posture of power infused with gentleness, patience, empathy, and long-suffering. The police undoubtedly possess significant power and deal with difficult people in stressful circumstances, which makes meekness an essential quality that must inform the duty of peacekeeping.

When a Christian form of Kant's imperative is applied to the police context, prudent peacekeeping emerges as the essential duty of the police, one that must be informed by the *imago Dei*, reconciliation, and meekness. Thus, our new police ethic demands that officers in all circumstances *keep the peace by the most peaceable means feasible,* committing to always *respect the dignity of all people* and orienting their hearts and actions toward *reconciliation* through a *gentle and patient exercise of power.* This is the true ethical north of policing.[17]

Officers must be guided morally by a duty to keep the peace in their community of respected members through judicious and conciliatory means. Inside every human heart is a longing for peace, a longing to be valued, and a longing for justice. The ethic of duty reflects these inner longings where all reasonable people recognize the police must be moral agents who value all people regardless of color or creed and pursue peace and justice without abusing power. Whether Christian, Buddhist, Muslim, atheist, or any other religion or view, I believe this ethic can resonate with us all.

LEADERSHIP AND CHARACTER UNDER PRESSURE

Police officers regularly encounter dynamic situations that can quickly become dangerous. Many times, adrenaline can fuel poor and even unethical responses. In the heat of these difficulties, officers need leaders who can reliably guide them. There's no time to plot a response plan during heated exchanges. The moral character of the leader will be the primary factor providing direction to officers on scene.

I experienced one of these situations one early morning over twenty years ago. I was parked across from a local African American nightclub around 2:30 a.m. during what had been a quiet summer night. Suddenly, several gunshots disrupted the silence. The shots appeared to be coming from the alley behind the bar. To make matters worse, the crowd was exiting the nightclub at that exact moment. I grabbed my shotgun and ran from my cruiser toward the alley, notifying my fellow officers over the radio of the shots fired. Most of the nearly three hundred people in the bar had exited at the time of the gunshots. As I tried to make my way into the alley, the crowd was running toward me, frantically trying to get away from the shooter. People were screaming and, in their panic, had difficulty avoiding me as I desperately tried to reach the scene of the gunfire. When I finally arrived on scene, a male stood in the alley under a streetlight. As soon as he saw me, he turned and ran in the opposite direction.

I gave chase. My heart was pumping hard from running in my full police gear while carrying a shotgun—not to mention the adrenaline from the very real fear that the man would shoot me. We ran for a few hundred yards and circled behind a building directly across from the nightclub. I lost sight of him as he turned the corner and though I could hear sirens as other officers began arriving, I knew if I waited for backup the man would likely be long gone. So I slowed to tactically navigate the corner of the building with my shotgun leading the way. I made it behind the building, and saw the man jump into the driver's seat of a parked SUV with three other males in the vehicle. I ran to the driver's side and raised my shotgun, yelling for everyone to raise their hands. All the men complied while beginning to throw small amounts of an illegal narcotic out the open windows. Around the same time, eight other officers arrived and we were able to secure the men in the vehicle without incident.

The parking lot where I arrested the men was the primary lot for the nightclub. Many people tried to get to their vehicles but were unable to do so because our police cars were blocking their way. Given the situation, we had not yet addressed the need to let people access their cars and leave. After about twenty minutes, a young African American woman in her twenties walked up to one of the officers on scene. Clearly pregnant, she asked the officer when she would be able to get to her car. The officer confronted her with a tirade of profanity, letting her know she was not a priority. Feeling disrespected, she replied, "If you're going to talk to me that way, you might as well take me to jail," punctuating her statement with the same demeanor and language used by the officer.

The officer told her she was under arrest and ordered her to turn around and place her hands behind her back. She looked frustrated and annoyed but complied. While attempting to handcuff her, the officer grabbed her roughly and twisted her arm awkwardly behind her back. Reacting to the discomfort, she pulled away, broke loose from his hold, and faced him to let him know he was hurting her arm. The arresting officer and a backup officer quickly drew their Tasers pointing the red laser sight on her chest and stomach. At this point, I stepped between her and the two officers and yelled, "Guys! She's pregnant!" I turned to her, looked her in her eyes, and gently asked, "Please turn around and do what he says." She complied and was placed in handcuffs.

I don't mean to paint myself as any kind of hero here. Being part of that debacle fills me with regret to this day. Years later, I became a supervisor and thought back many times on how I would have handled that incident differently, which provokes the question, Where was the supervisor during this incident? Certainly, it's a critically important question, especially since this chapter is focused on moral leadership.

So where was the supervisor?

He was standing right there on scene. He was the other officer pointing the Taser at the pregnant woman.

Given the dynamic, quickly evolving, and emotionally charged nature of police work, a leader's character is essential. What already exists inside comes out under stress. The moral compass has already been set firmly in his character, and the dynamic situation will expose whether the compass is pointed at true north. When there is no time for contemplation, emotional balancing, and hindsight responses, moral character determines the day. The character of leaders must be shaped by a leadership model and ethic that emphasize the depth of character and integrity needed for a law enforcement leader. As we will see in the next chapter, culture change begins with the leader—a servant-shepherd guided by an ethic of duty.

CHAPTER 8

TRANSFORMATION THROUGH LEADERSHIP

CREATING A NEW CULTURE OF SERVANTHOOD

A PERSON'S PRESENCE can be calming or provoking. The same is true of police officers. Some of them can provoke violent responses, their very presence almost ensuring some type of conflict. Unfortunately, even when officers realize a colleague exemplifies this combative persona, they usually tolerate the behavior. It's simply countercultural to submit a formal internal complaint.

I worked with officers like this. One escalated simmering incidents into full-scale riots on multiple occasions. Although he was at the center of several incidents, no action was ever taken against him. I dreaded working with him and even canceled him as backup, choosing to handle potentially volatile situations alone. Sadly, I had a greater fear that he would provoke a violent response than the potential of being outnumbered in a dangerous situation.

However, there were other officers who had the opposite effect. Their presence calmed situations and almost always helped to bring a peaceful conclusion. I had the privilege of serving under a sergeant that epitomized this tendency. He was an African American man who was undoubtedly counter-cultural. To this day, he is one of the leaders I respect most.

One summer night, we responded to a disturbance at a pri-marily African American nightclub. When I arrived on scene, people were pouring out of the bar. There were fights all around me, and the crowd had started to encircle the street. I felt helpless and fearful, realizing that if the crowd turned on me, there was nothing I could do. Some of the people were angry and not exactly police friendly. In the middle of the melee, my sergeant arrived. His presence immediately calmed me, as I knew I could trust his guidance. He spoke respectfully to the crowd and encouraged non-hostile people to please leave so we could help those in need. The crowd responded to his peaceful presence and large numbers of them simply departed. We then were able to calm some of the more hostile members of the crowd until only of few of the biggest agitators remained. Losing support from the crowd, they left as well. Within minutes a potentially riotous and dangerous situation was re-duced to an empty, peaceful parking lot.

Coincidently, I had a civilian observer with me that night. Without practical knowledge or expertise concerning the police, he recognized the amazing leadership of the sergeant. He said, "If that guy would not have been here, many people may have been hurt and maybe even us. I hope the department realizes what an asset that guy is." Unfortunately, the police department did not. In fact, his career was characterized by conflict with the higher leadership and was plagued by unofficial punishments, like being assigned to positions that limited his influence. Nonetheless, this sergeant illustrates the potential for servant-shepherd leaders to bring peace to their officers and communities.

TARGETING THE INTERNAL PROBLEM

I've demonstrated how police culture contributes to social distance between officers and racial minorities, leading to the dehumanization of minority groups and resulting in the abuse of power in the form of police brutality. I also reviewed the leadership and organizational structure in law enforcement establishing that the same pattern of social distance, dehumanization, and power abuse exists in police leaders toward officers. Therefore, police leaders model and thereby contribute to the disposition and behaviors in officers that can result in police brutality.

As a result, a new leadership model is needed that can be incorporated into the organizational structure of law enforcement and mitigate the problem of social distance, dehumanization, and the abuse of power. In chapter six, we constructed a new model of leadership—the servant-shepherd model—that rectifies the shortcomings of servant leadership in law enforcement. Essentially, the Christian worldview and a holistic Christian leadership model, reflected in Christ-centered followership, provided a foundation for servant leadership that can be synthesized into a clear and applicable leadership model for law enforcement.

Servant-shepherd leadership is authentically Christian yet applicable in the context of law enforcement for Christians and non-Christians alike. As we will see, servant-shepherd leadership and the new ethic of duty can address the internal contributing factors related to police culture—social distance, dehumanization, and abuse of power—and mitigate the problem of police brutality. Since I'm arguing that this leadership model and ethic can change police culture, we need to understand culture in general and general principles of cultural change.

Leadership and organizational change are distinct but related concepts. To truly change an organization through leadership, it's essential to understand how leadership changes an organization. Therefore, connecting leadership with a method for organizational change is necessary. To mitigate the problem of police brutality, we need revolutionary change. W. Warner Burke defines revolutionary change as a shift in the "deep structure" of the organization as a result of acute external pressure.[1] The deep structure includes the organizational culture and the foundational aspects of an organization,[2] and if the deep structure (organizational culture) is changed then this authentic change manifests in mission change.[3] Essentially, the heart of the organization (culture) is changed, and it is now reoriented toward a new end or mission.

Changing the culture, however, first requires understanding the nature of organizational culture. Edgar H. Schein posits that culture consists of three identifiable levels. The first level consists of "artifacts" or observable behaviors. The next level consists of "beliefs and values," and the deepest level

consists of "basic underlying assumptions."[4] Cultural behaviors are shaped by the beliefs and values upheld by the
basic underlying assumptions. To truly change culture, basic
underlying assumptions at the deepest level must be impacted.[5] To change police culture, we have to reach the deepest
level, or the underlying assumptions, supporting the beliefs
and values that inspire behaviors.

For instance, smoking was an acceptable practice in public
for decades, and secondhand smoke was not considered a real
problem in our culture. Although there was some understanding of the negative effects, the underlying assumption
among the public was that it really wasn't a dire matter. So,
smoking continued in theaters, on buses and planes, and in
restaurants. Today, however, the underlying assumption that
secondhand smoke is not harmful has been thoroughly de-
bunked. People believe it to be harmful and value smoke-free
environments. Prohibitions against smoking in public places
are the behavior that rests on the changed assumptions.

The nature of cultural change seems to indicate that the
pathway to cultural change starts with the underlying assumptions. Although authentic cultural change does require
changing the deepest level, ironically, the pathway to cultural
change actually starts with the artifacts or the behaviors.
Burke notes that change begins by targeting behaviors.[6]
Expressly, leaders cultivate cultural change by targeting behaviors directly related to erroneous underlying assumptions.

While the assumptions about secondhand smoke are drastically different today compared to American culture in the
1940s, the pathway to change was not facilitated by flooding

Americans with scholarly articles. Instead, leaders in the medical field and society addressed behaviors directly and primarily. Doctors encouraged their patients to stop smoking, television and radio prohibited tobacco advertisements, movies and media no longer promoted smoking as culturally desired or acceptable, institutions and organizations banned smoking on their property, and insurance companies penalized smokers when it came to premiums. This is not to suggest that beliefs, values, and underlying assumptions should not be directly targeted through education or other means, but it is to say that while challenging assumptions, beliefs, and values directly is helpful and needed, the primary focus for cultural change is directed toward the behaviors that rest upon the beliefs and assumptions. When leaders strategically target the behaviors inspired by faulty beliefs and assumptions, they recognize the most effective pathway to changing values and assumptions is through behavior or artifacts.

CHANGING POLICE CULTURE

The pattern of social distance, dehumanization, and power abuse is best understood through the three levels of culture. Police culture promotes the belief that police leaders possess intrinsic power, making them superior to officers. These beliefs are predicated on dangerous assumptions related to humanity and power, resulting in toxic leadership behaviors. The same assumptions, values, and behaviors can exist in officers and be directed toward the community, particularly the African American community. Therefore, to mitigate the problem of power abuse in the form of police brutality, police culture must be changed so that police leaders and officers no longer view themselves as separate from, superior to, and possessing intrinsic power over the community. However, as we saw previously, to reach the underlying assumptions, leaders must begin by targeting behaviors. So, we must target the specific behaviors rooted in the most concerning assumptions, beliefs, and values of police culture.

So how can we effectively target the most concerning behaviors in police culture? James M. Kouzes and Barry Z. Posner show us the way: "Exemplary leader behavior makes a profoundly positive difference in people's commitment and motivation, their work performance, and the success of the organization."[7] Thus, exemplary leadership is predicated on how leaders lead. Kouzes and Posner recommend five practices: "Model the way, inspire a shared vision, challenge the process, enable others to act, and encourage the heart."[8] These provide a general methodology related to organizational change that corresponds with the servant-shepherd model.[9] In other words, these practices furnish the servant-shepherd model with a general method to influence officers effectively and to promote organizational change. The servant-shepherd leader is *present* with officers, *protecting* and *providing* for them to *model, inspire, challenge, enable,* and *encourage* them toward becoming servant-shepherds themselves. These guiding leadership principles can be used to take aim at specific behaviors that will target the dangerous assumptions and values in police culture that can lead to revolutionary change.

MODEL THE WAY

Therefore, servant-shepherd leaders must "model the way."[10] They must be present with officers—listening, aware, empathizing, and building community—to model the behaviors that communicate they are one with their community of officers. Additionally, they are protecting—using persuasion and not coercion, conceptualizing, and using foresight—to model the behaviors that communicate the judicious and benevolent use of power and further the mission of justice and peace. They also provide for their officers by modeling behaviors that support the core principles of the servant-shepherd model while highlighting connection with their officers. As a servant-shepherd—present, protecting, and providing—they model the familial relationship and share a journey of difficulty and hope with their officers, who are equally valuable parts of a mission that involves suffering.

In short, their behaviors model the values and principles of the servant-shepherd model—leaders are united with and equal to the community, power is used judiciously and benevolently—contradicting the police culture's dangerous beliefs and assumptions. Most importantly, the servant-shepherd leader demonstrates they are a follower first, committed to operating with integrity, care, and self-control.

Looking back on my law enforcement career, I am thankful to have served in a community policing unit. When the unit began it was supervised by a sergeant who was counter-cultural—the same sergeant who calmed the near riot. He was personal with people, and it was not uncommon for him to know their families and personal stories. Not only did I see that he was different, but we also engaged in conversation over the years. In those moments, I began to understand how he thought about policing. Not only did he teach me by example, but he took the time to clearly explain to me why he acted differently.

INSPIRE A SHARED VISION AND CHALLENGE THE PROCESS

Therefore, it is important to understand that "inspiring a shared vision" and "challenging the process" are supported by leading by example, and a leader's example must be complemented by explicit teaching.[11] The mission of justice and peace must be taught, not just modeled. The police mission remains largely focused on enforcement, and for the mission to change, servant-shepherd leaders must explain the value of making justice and peace the primary mission for law enforcement. Additionally, the shepherd framework must be explained. Officers must understand their function as being present with the community to protect and provide as well as their familial relationship to the community as that of fellow redeemed sojourners, living stones, and suffering servants. Officers are one with their community and are to act as servant-shepherd officers. The officers are the servants and shepherds of their communities—present, protecting, providing—sharing a journey of difficulty and hope with the community who are equally valuable parts of a shared mission that involves suffering.

The shepherd's modeling and teaching are essential. Nonetheless, the connective aspect of the shepherd framework or the servant-shepherd leader's relationship with officers is also paramount. The mission of justice and peace is largely dependent on connecting with the community in a relationship defined by the shepherd leadership framework. Officers and people of color have suffered together in this turbulent journey and must come together as redeemed sojourners who acknowledge the pain of the past but emphasize hope in a new future where officers and the community press forward as living stones down a difficult road that will require change and suffering. Without emphasizing a new relationship, the heart of servant-shepherd leadership will not match the action. Therefore, the actions of the servant-shepherd leader become effective in reforming officers only when that leader has a healthy relationship with their officers. The shepherd framework addresses both aspects: action and relationship.

Clearly, the principles, practices, and defining relationships of servant-shepherd leadership cannot simply be modeled. Servant-shepherd leadership calls for a new vision and challenges the typical police models of leadership. The sophistication of the model necessitates that leaders explicitly teach it while leading as servants and shepherds. In doing so, servant-shepherd leaders can inspire a new vision and challenge the old process.

ENABLE OTHERS TO ACT AND ENCOURAGE THE HEART

In the law enforcement world, we often think leaders should always be in the front. Unfortunately, I cannot think of many instances where a ranking leader purposely put me in a position to lead unless it was a task they wanted to avoid. However, I had an experience as a police chaplain that taught me how important it is for leaders to purposely place their followers in the front. On one occasion, a family reached out to me to preach at a funeral service for a tragic incident. Their pastor was unavailable, and they needed help. I had never spoke at a funeral service and felt unqualified for this solemn occasion. I called my pastor to see if he could speak at the service in my place. He listened to me as I explained the situation, and after a long pause he told me something I'll never forget: "I am more than willing to do it, but this is something you should do." He recognized he was more qualified and experienced to handle this delicate situation, yet he still knew it was best that I preach at the service. The family had called for me, and I was positioned on the front line of this situation and needed to be the one to respond. So it is with officers. The supervisor cannot always be there, and officers are on the front lines of service. The servant-shepherd leader knows this and is willing to step back so officers can practice what they have seen modeled and taught. This is an indispensable part of leadership that prepares and matures officers to provide genuine leadership in their communities.

Police leaders must "enable others to act."[12] Officers must be placed in situations to act as servants and shepherds. Calls for service create opportunities every day, but certain contexts can help officers develop the heart and actions behind the servant-shepherd model. Whenever possible, servant-shepherd leaders should defer to officers when dealing with racial minorities in crisis, allowing officers the opportunity to act as servants and shepherds. Additionally, servant-shepherd leaders should purposely position officers at community events where they can interact as one with the community. Being intentional about shaping and influencing officers requires utilizing contexts that help officers grow into servants and shepherds.

Providing these opportunities for officers to succeed also gives the servant-shepherd leader opportunities to "encourage the heart."[13] When officers demonstrate the heart and actions of servant-shepherd leadership, the servant-shepherd leader seizes the opportunity to express appreciation to the officer and celebrate the new values represented by the servant-shepherd model.[14] Nonetheless, officers will always fall short at one point or another. Therefore, the servant-shepherd leader will have to take corrective action. For instance, if an officer talks condescendingly to community members, they must be corrected, but the servant-shepherd leader corrects as a family member and protector. They identify the behavior as unacceptable and remind the officer of their identity as a servant-shepherd leader of the community. The behavior is targeted, yet the beliefs and values underlying the servant-shepherd model are reinforced, and the officer is encouraged to behave accordingly.

Incorporating Kouzes and Posner's method of leadership into the servant-shepherd model maximizes its potential to cultivate revolutionary change in police culture whereby police departments can be fundamentally transformed. The foundational principles of the servant-shepherd model support the shepherd framework (action and relationship) to be specifically applied in a deeply meaningful and strategic manner leading to revolutionary change.

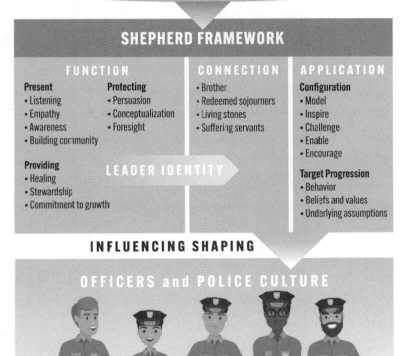

FOUNDATIONAL PRINCIPLES

1 Follower first   **2** One with community of officers
3 Judicious and benevolent use of power   **4** Mission of peace and justice

DEFINING
SERVANT LEADERSHIP CHARACTERISTICS

SHEPHERD FRAMEWORK

FUNCTION

Present
- Listening
- Empathy
- Awareness
- Building community

Protecting
- Persuasion
- Conceptualization
- Foresight

Providing
- Healing
- Stewardship
- Commitment to growth

LEADER IDENTITY

CONNECTION
- Brother
- Redeemed sojourners
- Living stones
- Suffering servants

APPLICATION

Configuration
- Model
- Inspire
- Challenge
- Enable
- Encourage

Target Progression
- Behavior
- Beliefs and values
- Underlying assumptions

INFLUENCING SHAPING

OFFICERS and POLICE CULTURE

Figure 8.1. Servant-shepherd model application

THE POWER OF TRUE CHARACTER

Jesus led by example, and his words and actions aligned. His life served as a foundation for his sermons, and even when he was outwardly stripped of any signs of who he was, his inner character continued to testify to the truth. After being scourged and hung on the cross, his physical appearance was so distorted as to make him unrecognizable. What man looks like a king while being crucified? Yet who he was could not be eclipsed even by the humiliation of a crucifixion.

The thief hanging next to Jesus should have seen just another criminal knocking on death's door. Instead, even in Jesus' state, he recognized the King of the universe. Speaking to the other criminal crucified next to Jesus, he said, "Do you not fear God, since you are under the same sentence of condemnation? And we indeed justly, for we are receiving the due reward of our deeds; but this man has done nothing wrong" (Luke 23:40-41). Then he looked to Jesus and said, "Jesus, remember me when you come into your kingdom" (v. 42). With every sign of his kingship stripped away, Jesus' identity, character, and authority remained unmistakable.

Jesus' reputation preceded him, and his character radiated beyond all outward circumstances. In Jesus' presence, the thief had to admit his guilt and repent. Surely, had he lived, he would have been a different man. Although a police leader cannot be Jesus, they can be like Jesus in this: their character precedes them, and their presence shines the light of integrity on those who they lead. A servant-shepherd leader can impact a culture as an embodied representative of a new leadership model and ethic that shines a light into the darkness that is police culture. Even in the most difficult and demeaning circumstances, their leadership and character can be unmistakable, shaping a new culture that can support new strategies for peaceful communities.

CHAPTER 9

A NEW STRATEGY OF PEACE

PROCEDURAL JUSTICE
AND COMMUNITY POLICING

AS A ROOKIE OFFICER I spent the majority of my first three years working night shift. We were an enforcement-driven police department at the time. "Good police officers" did not accept disrespectful behavior from citizens—ever—and made vast amounts of misdemeanor arrests as well as felony arrests, which were considered high-quality arrests. Furthermore, the solution to almost every disturbance was simple: arrest someone or even everyone. If we encountered large groups arguing, we didn't deescalate. Instead, we started "locking people up."[1] If we made a traffic stop and a person acted in a way that was considered disrespectful, there was a good chance that traffic stop would end with some type of arrest. If someone began to yell or vent their frustration with us, more likely than not, they were going to jail.

I was often the transport and booking officer, which meant picking up arrestees from other officers and transporting them to jail for booking and processing. Veteran officers would turn over an arrestee and say, "The usual two." This meant that the person was charged with disorderly conduct and disorderly conduct persisting—in other words, contempt of cop. On many nights, I would enter the booking room and not leave until the end of my shift. Officers brought in people one after another all night long, many of them arrested for disorderly conduct and similar offenses. Clearly the focus was on arrests and not community relations, and unfortunately at that time, this approach was considered good police work. Through my early experiences as a police officer, I uncritically accepted that our mission and purpose was enforcement—perhaps not our sole purpose, but unquestionably the most important one.

By mission, I am not referring to formal mission statements in police policy that are likely nothing more than platitudes that do not accurately reflect the purpose and intentions of line officers in the field. By mission, I mean the true conception of what the police do—which for many is to enforce the law. However, just shy of three years into my police career, I had a significant experience that began to shift my understanding of the police mission. I was assigned to a three-man community policing unit that patrolled a large housing project in the city. I had no idea what community policing was at the time, and I assumed I would be part of a hard-charging, enforcement-driven unit.[2] Working with the two veteran officers in the unit, I was surprised at their focus. They were more concerned with solving problems and building relationships. I initially thought they were lazy police officers, but my perception began to change as we continued working together.

We started a wrestling team for the underprivileged youth in the housing development. The housing authority donated money to buy them the necessary equipment, and we partnered with the local high school for a practice facility. Through coaching, I developed relationships with my wrestlers and their families. Additionally, since I was working in a single development and not the entire city, I formed relationships with the people who lived there. As I responded to repeated calls for service and encountered the same people daily, my changed perception was a natural consequence. Through these experiences, I started to question whether our mission as police officers should be primarily enforcement. I began to empathize more when I encountered an angry citizen, and I understood that while arresting the person might end the immediate conflict, it would not solve the issue. In fact, an arrest only created bigger problems for the person and further compromised their relationship with the police.

My interactions with the community members helped me understand that problem-solving approaches involving community partnerships—although more difficult and time-consuming—had far greater potential to make the community safer than enforcement-centric strategies. Although the mission of enforcement is simple, expedient, and easily quantifiable, the police should reconsider the long-term repercussions. What will we do with our statistics and quotas when our cities burn due to civil unrest because of the years we spent compromising our relationship with our communities? Clearly defining the mission of policing can be difficult, but adjusting our understanding is paramount if we truly want peace in our communities.

CHANGING THE MISSION AND STRATEGY

True organizational change and police reform will manifest in revolutionary change, resulting in authentic mission change, and a changed police department needs a new strategy consistent with its reformed culture and mission. In considering police reform, Radley Balko recognizes this relationship and argues both police culture and enforcement philosophies must change, specifically noting the need to adopt community policing.[3] He's right, but he focuses on external measures for implementation, such as training, accountability through policy, and disciplining officers.[4] Although they are needed, without police leaders embodying a new culture that inspires cultural reform, these external measures alone will fall short.

As we've seen, police culture can usurp formal policies and training. So true reform requires more than policy changes and attempts at implementing community policing. One of the reasons community policing has failed to inaugurate reform is because of "the police culture that resists engaging with the community and emphasizing prevention and positive interaction."[5] Essentially, the current police culture and leadership naturally support militant-style enforcement over community engagement. Therefore, to incorporate community-oriented strategies, the leadership and police culture must change first. For many police departments today, community policing is a small group of officers who act like blinds on a window. The public can only see the veneer of community policing and are unable to look through the window into the true nature of the police department. Perhaps police departments are not intentionally deceptive, but the public is nonetheless fooled.

The servant-shepherd leadership model and ethic are predicated on the reality that internal cultural reform must be primary. Once servant-shepherd leaders have cultivated servant-shepherd officers, the culture is ripe for embracing a community-oriented strategy beyond the veneer of nominal appropriation, one that truly supports the mission of justice and peace. To that end, we will turn our attention to a strategy that aligns with cultural reform and the mission of peace.

THE PROCEDURAL JUSTICE MODEL OF POLICE LEGITIMACY

The procedural justice model of police legitimacy is a promising *philosophy* in policing, particularly urban policing. Rod K. Brunson and Jacinta M. Gau explain that it

> emphasizes the importance of professional, respectful, and equitable treatment of all citizens during every police-public contact. It rejects an "us versus them" mindset and instead focuses on the social-psychological impacts that encounters with police exert upon citizens. Perhaps most critical to the matter of policing disadvantaged, predominantly-minority urban areas, the procedural justice model highlights the importance of individuals' perceptions of themselves as valued members of society as conveyed through the way in which they are treated by officers. Rational legitimacy depends upon consensus; people

must feel that they are part of the system, that irrespective of their race, gender, age, or socioeconomic status, they are a member of the "majority" in the societal sense.[6]

The model stresses trust and public cooperation whereby officers make impartial decisions with courtesy to gain compliance from the public who comply because they recognize police legitimacy.[7] Public cooperation, not force, is the primary means for the police to gain compliance, a metric Robert Peel would surely celebrate. Furthermore, Brunson and Gau assert that procedural justice is a "cornerstone philosophy," underscoring community support, cultivating public trust and strong community relations as essential for peacekeeping, and rejecting "aggressive, intrusive policing" that alienates the community and "impedes police effectiveness."[8] Ultimately, the procedural justice model is a philosophy predicated on community justice and peacekeeping, not military-style enforcement.

The servant-shepherd model and ethic correspond with the procedural justice model of police legitimacy in several ways. First, the emphasis on "professional, respectful, and equitable treatment of all citizens" directly relates to the foundational principle of being a follower first of the high ethical standards of law enforcement and being one with the community. Officers—as followers first—respect and care for everyone because they are one with their community. Second, as a servant-shepherd, the officer is listening, empathizing, intent on healing, and committed to the growth of their fellow peers. They seriously consider the "social-psychological impacts that encounters with police exert upon citizens" and are deeply concerned about "individuals' perceptions of themselves as valued members." Third, the servant-shepherd officer participates as a redeemed fellow sojourner alongside their community on a mission of justice and peace where everyone is valuable. Thus, they desire that every member of the community "feels that they are part of the system."[9]

The procedural justice model of police legitimacy corresponds with core principles and practices of the servant-shepherd model and ethic. As a result, it can serve as the *fundamental philosophy* for police departments where police culture has been impacted by the servant-shepherd model of leadership and ethic. A police culture shaped by the servant-shepherd model organically supports the procedural justice model of police legitimacy as a foundational philosophy.

COMMUNITY POLICING

The *methodology* of community policing emphasizes personal interactions with citizens, crime prevention, and limited geographical locations for officers so they can develop bonds with the community.[10] Officers are consistently assigned to specific neighborhoods and endeavor to prevent crime by cultivating relationships and partnerships with the community. Officers concentrate on positive interactions that help offset the necessary and inevitable enforcement practices of policing.[11] Furthermore, officers actively seek out partnerships to solve problems in the community by addressing underlying conditions.[12]

Community policing naturally aligns with the servant-shepherd model. The emphasis on face-to-face relations is consistent with the servant-shepherd model's focus on presence that incorporates listening, empathizing, developing awareness, and building community. Additionally, the prevention emphasis in community policing reflects the principle that power is to be used judiciously and benevolently. Lastly, community policing's emphasis on partnerships and community correlates with the servant-shepherd's principle of community oneness and the function of protecting and providing as a family member on a shared journey.

Although I have presented the road to reform as linear— change leadership, change culture, support a new strategy— practically speaking, leaders and police reformers would not wait until the culture is changed before implementing the procedural justice model of police legitimacy and community policing. A reform effort would require immediately changing the strategy. Nonetheless, reformers should recognize that the new strategy will never become fully effective until the leadership changes the culture.

THE EMPOWERED SERVANT-SHEPHERD OFFICER

Servant-shepherd leaders ultimately endeavor to develop servant-shepherd officers by instilling the values, practices, and relational understanding represented in the servant-shepherd model and ethic. As a result, officers and eventually the police culture adopt a different perspective that resists oppressive strategies. The new culture facilitates the implementation and preservation of the procedural justice model of police legitimacy and community policing, and when servant-shepherd leaders institute this philosophy and methodology departmentally, the servant-shepherd officer is fully empowered to engage in the mission of justice and peace.

PRESENT WITH THEIR PEOPLE

Regardless of race, color, or creed, the servant-shepherd officer recognizes all people are intrinsically valuable and share in the unified mission of justice and peace.[13] The servant-shepherd officer cannot be a distant figure set against the community as an enforcer because they recognize that identity isolates the police from the community. The servant-shepherd officer enters the community, refusing to accept the "myth of race" and recognizing the unity and value of every person as part of "the human race."[14] Present with their people, they are intent on listening and empathizing. In doing so, they grow self-aware and community minded, and their understanding enables them to build community relationships and partnerships. Therefore, the procedural justice model of police legitimacy and community policing provide the structure to empower the servant-shepherd officer who is present in their community.

PROTECTING

The servant-shepherd officer is committed to "sustaining and safeguarding" their people.[15] They safeguard the community and rescue people who are in danger.[16] Protection has a clear application when it comes to victims of crime and those who call the police for help. However, one may question if protection applies to people who are arrested or cited. In other words, is the servant-shepherd officer's role as a protector applicable to enforcement? From the servant-shepherd perspective, enforcement is not a practice intended to punish or to incarcerate but is understood as a function necessary for the peace of the entire community.[17] Enforcement, therefore, should be understood as a practice that can better the community and promote peace. It must not be used to target and punish aberrant citizens but should be applied as one specific function of the greater mission of peacekeeping.

Enforcement can be an important means for the police to protect their communities. Unfortunately, some people are violent and dangerous and must be arrested to protect the community and promote peace. Nonetheless, the servant-shepherd officer realizes the need for fearfully and judiciously wielding the power delegated to them by the people to arrest as a good steward of the community. Incarcerated people are also members of the community who should be treated with dignity and respect, and the arrest of a community member is intended to protect the society to which the arrested person will eventually return. As a result, the servant-shepherd officer relies on persuasion, and physical force is a last resort for effecting an arrest. Arrests are made as a protective function for the entire community, even those arrested. Additionally, the prevention focus of community policing enables them to minimize enforcement as they conceptualize and exercise foresight in preventing crime and disorder. The procedural justice model of police legitimacy and community policing complement the servant-shepherd model empowering officers to protect the entire community, even those who must be arrested.

PROVIDING

The servant-shepherd officer is also a provider whose function includes practices outside traditional law enforcement. They seek ways to provide for the community that will improve the lives of the people and promote peace. There are virtually no limits to this function, for the servant-shepherd officer is motivated by compassion for the community.[18] They see the needs of the helpless and are compelled to respond in any way possible.

Many young men in urban communities need additional support to avoid the traps of urban poverty. Police officers can build relationships with these young men and provide needed support and guidance alongside pastors and community leaders. There is a desperate need for caring men who can help build young men into men of integrity and honor, men committed to living respectful and peaceful lives.[19]

Additionally, as a provider, the servant-shepherd officer focuses on the healing and growth of their community. As a redeemed sojourner, they remember the past, thereby understanding the great need for healing. Therefore, they are not afraid to apologize for law enforcement's past to promote healing in the present. This view may be challenging for many officers, but the servant-shepherd officer, as a redeemed sojourner, recognizes they are no longer bound by the past and seizes the opportunity to take responsibility and apologize to promote healing in their community.

This can be a powerful tool for reconciliation. Shortly after the death of Michael Brown, the tension in our community was palpable. An older African American woman who I knew to be a Christian approached me and let me know how angry the community was—especially the young people. I think she expected a defensive or even negative response from me. I did not respond that way; instead I simply said, "Well, they have a lot to be angry about. I'm sorry for the way so many in our community have been treated." Her eyes welled with tears, and she hugged me. Servant-shepherd officers are fully committed to the growth of their brothers and sisters and walk the path of shared suffering to promote justice and peace.

Servant-shepherd officers, therefore, should be compelled by compassion to respond in unconventional ways to provide for their communities, like coaching, mentoring, or volunteering at local organizations. This type of commitment, of course, is not mandatory, but as officers begin to see themselves as one with the community, many will be motivated to serve beyond their eight-hour shift. The providing function—consistent with community policing—emphasizes positive encounters that can substantially soften the impact of enforcement actions. The procedural justice model of police legitimacy and community policing clearly complement the servant-shepherd model of leadership empowering officers to be unconventional providers.

When we tie together the procedural justice model of police legitimacy, community policing, and the servant-shepherd model of leadership and ethic with the servant-shepherd officer policing the community, we have a synchronous philosophy, methodology, leadership model, ethic, and officer model. In simple terms, the thinking and doing of a police department at all levels is laser focused on serving to bring peace and justice to the community.

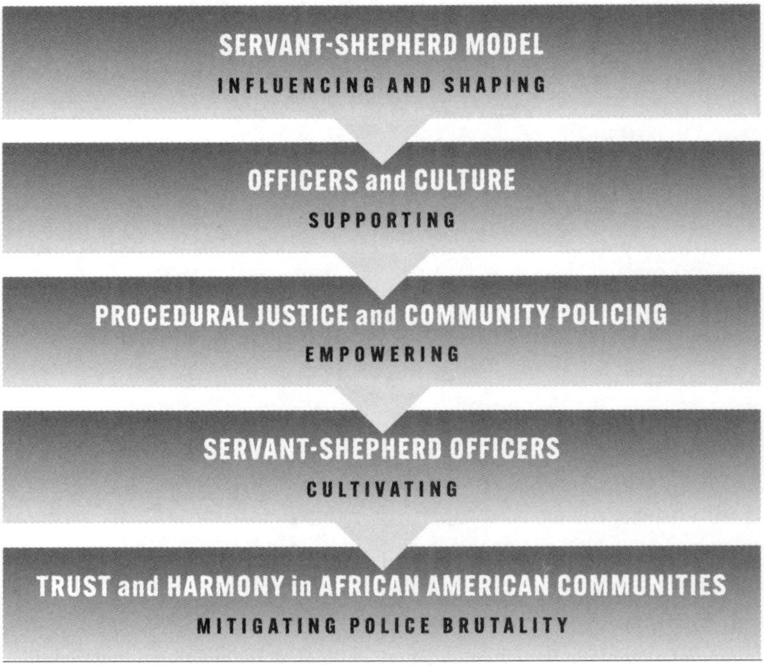

Figure 9.1. Servant-shepherd model of leadership transformation progression

CHAPTER 10

IMPACTING A HURTING DEMOGRAPHIC

BUILDING POSITIVE IDENTITIES

AS WE THINK ABOUT THE RELATIONSHIP of thinking and doing, identity surfaces as a paramount conceptualization. If the police are shaped to think like servant-shepherds through our leadership model and ethic, then they will act as servant-shepherds. Therefore, the servant-shepherd model is more than a model—it is an identity. Thinking and action align because they naturally flow from an identity.

When Jesus began his ministry in the first century, the Jews were looking for a messiah, and the various Jewish groups had different conceptions of the Messiah's identity. One example is the Zealots, who believed the Messiah to be a coming warlord who would defeat the Romans and reestablish Israel as a ruling kingdom. Therefore, they identified as soldiers and insurrectionists participating in civil acts of violence as they prepared for a war with the Romans. Convincing the

Zealots to act differently would have been impossible. Their actions were perfectly aligned with their identity. To change their actions, one would have to first change who they believed themselves to be

So it is with the police. Like the Zealots, who misunderstood who they were as servants of the Messiah, the police misunderstand who they are and what they should do. They are not enforcers on a mission to take back our cities by fighting a war against the people. No, they are servant-shepherds of the people called to bring peace. They have forgotten their foundation in Peel, and like the Zealots, have drifted far from who they should be and what they should be doing. In this final chapter we will close by centralizing the importance of identity and relationship in the servant-shepherd's investment in the mission of peace.

THE DIVIDEND OF ANGER AND RESISTANCE— AN INVESTMENT IN OPPRESSION

If we consider the relationship between the police and the community, particularly the African American community, and determine how the police have *invested* in the community, we get an enlightening perspective.[1] Every action we take is an investment that pays some sort of dividend in the future. Sadly, the police were the enforcers of slave laws and Jim Crow laws, and that same spirit of oppression underlies the war on drugs; and today I believe that same spirit also underlies intelligence-led/zero-tolerance policing. Tragically, we must recognize that the actions of the police in the past echo a message of dominance and oppression into today's communities of color, one that is reinforced by intelligence-led/zero-tolerance policing. It should come as no surprise that this investment of oppression would engender anything but resistance.

I am not implying that people are not responsible for their actions, but I am acknowledging that we exist in a real world where our actions affect one another. Therefore, to truly understand the situation, we must realize the police and African American communities are in a relationship within a system. Consequently, police strategies and practices must take relationship and the system into account. This should lead the police to a more long-term analysis of existing practices. For instance, how has the war on drugs affected the African American community? Would it be a stretch to suggest that the investment made in the war on drugs has culminated in today's riots and civil unrest over incidents of police brutality? Acts of police violence and biased policing have made a substantial investment in the current dividend of community anguish and rebellion.

Given the dangerous police culture and ethic, it seems unlikely that any real, long-term relational or systems-wide analysis has taken place. I began my career during the war on drugs when crack cocaine was deemed the primary problem in our community. Although we did not have the same sophistication and precision that facilitates identifying problem areas as today's intelligence-led policing, as a rookie officer I was well aware of the areas deemed "the hood." Good officers spent most of their time in these areas, making traffic stops and initiating stop and frisk encounters. Eventually, these methods would result in locating cocaine, often in the form of a crack pipe.[2] The pipes usually belonged to addicts who were suffering from a serious problem. We would test the residue in the pipe and arrest the person for felony possession of cocaine, and our regular arrests were reported as success. However, I do not believe many police officers or departments at the time considered the broader message we were communicating or the long-term ramifications of our methods.

Today, with the heroin epidemic, when an addict is found overdosing or in possession of tools for using heroin, generally, no criminal charges result. Instead, they receive medical treatment. Although I believe this to be the correct response, why such disparity of practice? Perhaps we have learned from our mistakes as a society. This, of course, is an optimistic appraisal, for some believe the disparity of practice is due to racial factors—crack cocaine was considered a Black drug and heroin a White drug. The police practices that turned many drug-addicted people into felons no longer exist today when it comes to heroin, and I believe that reality has sent a message to the African American community that has had lasting consequences.

Officers and police departments need to think in terms of investment and development of the community, which should include those in serious need. From this perspective, urban adolescents naturally arise as a demographic of concern. Fortunately, I was able to spend three years as a school resource officer, where I interacted with urban adolescents daily, developing relationships with them in an environment where most of our encounters were positive. During that time, I coached wrestling and cultivated relationships with my wrestlers that enabled me to influence and shape them. One young man had experienced great difficulty in his life. His father was an alcoholic and largely absent and his mother was a cocaine addict. As he entered high school, he hoped to achieve some sense of normalcy through his studies and athletics, but his home life made this difficult. On one occasion, he awoke to find a drug dealer in his home with his mother. The confrontation resulted in a fight between the young man and the adult drug dealer. Yet in a matter of hours he was in a classroom, trying to function like the other students

Through wrestling, he was able to interact with me and other responsible and caring adults where we could mentor and shape him. He even developed friendships with my children. In this context, we could not ignore each other's humanity. This young man went on to graduate and join the military, and he and I have maintained a relationship ever since. These types of encounters are paramount to healing the racial divide and tearing down the cultural barriers. Without community-centered strategies, personal encounters are severely limited, and few opportunities exist for interacting in relational contexts. Instead of positive encounters, the police and urban youth only encounter each other on oppositional terms.

The police need to shed their utilitarian ethic and build a culture through leadership that emphasizes relationship and unity. I believe this will better position the police to promote and implement practices that take into consideration the system and our effect on each other. It will illuminate the reality that long-term relational investment strategies are necessary for true change in our police-community relationships.

Surely, police history has proven beyond all doubt that we will never enforce our way to peace.

RELATIONSHIP AND IDENTITY FORMATION

The previous chapters culminated in a general application of the servant-shepherd model and ethic. Certainly, the model needs to be applied, but as I mentioned, it is more than just a model. It is also an identity, one that can have an important impact on a particular demographic that needs positive encounters with the police.[3] In this chapter, we will be looking at the same problem in policing but from a distinct perspective—a relational systems and identity perspective. In doing so, we will not maintain the same general scope on racial minorities but will focus specifically on one important demographic—African American adolescents. I believe the police need to respond as servant-shepherds to a deep wound that has been formed by their history with African Americans with a focus on African American adolescents.

The United States of America has a rich history, yet slavery, segregation, and even the lynching tree are not ancient historical events. Instead, these sad realities are relatively recent occurrences that remain ingrained in the memories of many Americans, particularly African Americans.[4] The police, as the peacekeepers of our communities, were placed at the forefront of these regretful practices to enforce unjust laws and respond to protests and large-scale civil unrest.[5]

Because of this history and the contentious relationship that formed, the police and African Americans in urban communities often have contrasting identities. Malcom D. Holmes and Brad W. Smith argue that "police brutality is a grim symptom of intractable intergroup dynamics involving racial and ethnic minority citizens and police officers who patrol their neighborhoods."[6] Certainly, there are no simple solutions to this ongoing tension, but one consistent contributing factor has been the conflict of identity between the police and African Americans.[7] Bearing that in mind, identity formation is an important matter concerning law enforcement's ability to peacefully police African American communities. As we will see, negative interactions with the police help form negative identities and oppositional behaviors in African American adolescents. However, when police officers act as servant-shepherds, they can help develop positive identities in African American adolescents and promote peaceful interactions. I believe by focusing on cultivating positive identities in African American adolescents, we can further mitigate the problem of police brutality. Today's positive investment in this important demographic can lead to a future dividend of peaceful encounters.

THE LENS FOR ANALYSIS

Richard Lerner asserts, "Developmental systems models are at the cutting edge of theory in developmental science" and provide a frame for lifespan development.[8] We will use this "cutting edge theory" to analyze and adjust mindsets that may be impeding law enforcement's ability to keep the peace in African American communities. Identity development can be understood from the larger perspective of developmental systems theory. In fact, relational development systems theory has been identified as a helpful framework for understanding racial identity development in African American adolescents.[9] As a result, a relational development systems theory perspective that focuses on racial identity development can give us greater insight into the tension between the police and African American communities, specifically with African American adolescents.

Developmental systems theory (DST) is rooted in psychology and biology and explains developmental processes from the perspective that organisms and the environment interact as a complex system. The system consists of "dynamic interactions" between organisms and the environment that are mutually formative;[10] and relational developmental systems theory (RDST) is concerned with the influential relationship between the individual and the context as the locus to understand change and development. For our purposes, the technical language is not necessarily important, but understand that *development takes place in an individual as they exist in and interact with their environment.* This interactive exchange between individuals and environments is how we examine and understand the process of change in individuals.

Since personal development takes place in a relational system and our goal is for the police to help and not hinder African American adolescents, positive youth development (PYD) is an important RDST theory. PYD "seeks to understand and enhance the lives of diverse adolescents through engagement with key contexts in their ecology (for example families, schools, peer group, and out-of-school programs)."[11] So, RDST and PYD make clear that positive change is possible in adolescents, and we best understand how positive change can take place when we consider the relational nature of society and how community groups like the police interact with adolescents. Community groups that interact with adolescents, therefore, can hinder or contribute to the positive development of adolescents, but they cannot be neutral or inert. They will have some level of effect on the development of African American adolescents.

IDENTITY FORMATION

Harry E. Gardiner defines identity as "a person's self-definition as a separate and distinct individual, including behaviors, beliefs, and attitudes."[12] Adolescence is an important period where a person's identity is actively formed through an interactive process with the social environment.[13] During this time, young people have an emerging and defining identity, especially a racial identity.[14] Specific experiences, such as racial discrimination, can be powerfully formative.[15] Racial discrimination and negativity can be extremely harmful to one's overall racial identity when negative conceptions of racial minorities result in "internalized oppression," where adolescents accept the negative racial stereotype as factual and develop mistrust for White people.[16]

Internalized oppression in its fullest expression is nothing short of catastrophic.

The more insidious and damaging forms of internalized oppression are related to anger and rage, low private regard for one's group, a sense of hopelessness and defeatism, REC-related [racial, ethnic, and cultural] hypersensitivity (sensitivity to possible REC-related social rejection), and deep feelings of low self-worth linked to REC-related self-hatred. In addition to depression, low self-esteem, imbalance between negative and positive emotions, and impeded ego identity development, such negativity can lead to lifestyle problems (addiction, marital problems, sexual deviancy, etc.) that further compound one's situation.[17]

Therefore, contextual influences can have a significant impact on the racial identity formation of adolescents, and negative, prejudicial, and discriminatory treatment can have catastrophic effects on an adolescent's identity and life.

MMRI AND THE POLICE

The Multidimensional Model of Racial Identity (MMRI) is a dynamic theory specifically focused on African American racial identity formation, and it will help us get a better grasp of the importance of identity concerning the police and African American adolescents. MMRI consists of four dimensions: salience, centrality, regard, and ideology. Salience refers to the importance of a person's racial identity in a particular situation. Centrality concerns the normal or relatively stable conception of a person's racial identity. Regard relates to the extent that a person feels positively or negatively about their racial identity. Ideology encompasses the core beliefs and values that the person thinks should guide the behavior of persons that identify with the racial identity.[18]

The dimensions of regard and salience are particularly important for the police. Negative regard for African Americans by society and the police can be absorbed and accepted by African Americans themselves, and salience recognizes that certain contexts or situations can have a significant effect on racial identity because the interaction stresses the importance of a person's racial identity. Therefore, frequent, highly salient encounters with police officers who have a negative regard for African Americans (either personally or culturally/systemically) can significantly and negatively impact the identity assumed by African American adolescents. Most importantly for the police concerning peacekeeping, when negative regard and salience intersect, these types of encounters have great potential to provoke an angry and dangerous response in African American adolescents.[19] *Simply understood, police actions during encounters with African American youth will significantly impact their identity formation and behavior.*

THE POLICE AND AFRICAN AMERICANS

Now that we have a basic understanding of the relational nature of identity formation and the impact the police can have on African American adolescents, let's consider how the police have contributed to the identity formation of African American adolescents. The history provided in chapter one illustrated the contentious relationship between the police and the African American community as a whole. Nonetheless, African American adolescents were part of the larger community and experienced the same historical events. Additionally, given that adolescence is an influential period concerning identity formation, it could be argued that the sad history of police abuses was most impactful on African American adolescents.

The police have a specific identity related to values and norms unique to themselves that has been developed within police culture, and largely by the informal code. A particularly concerning aspect of the police identity that has been highlighted throughout this book is the us-them worldview.

African American adolescents in urban communities also have a social identity, and it is usually drastically different from that of the police.[20] Therefore, police officers can find it difficult to peacefully interact with African Americans in urban neighborhoods,[21] especially since African Americans tend to view the police with suspicion and fear.[22] They also tend to believe the police are untrustworthy, representatives of the White community, oppressors, and a real danger to their safety.[23] Due to the conflicting understandings that undergird the identities of African Americans and the police, an adversarial relationship has formed, and conflict is inevitable.[24]

THE POLICE AND THE IDENTIFY FORMATION OF AFRICAN AMERICAN ADOLESCENTS

The racial identity of African Americans assumes a prominent role in encounters with police officers, and if police officers have negative feelings toward African Americans, it can cultivate negative feelings in African Americans concerning themselves.[25] Since the police interact with African American adolescents at a critical point in their identity formation in a highly salient context, we understand that negative interactions with the police can contribute to the development of negative identities in African American adolescents.

Furthermore, these highly salient encounters can result in hostility toward the police, and the hostility can influence behavior.[26] Most concerning is that the resentment and hostility toward the police can manifest in contentious behavior with the potential for violence and death.[27] Sadly, African American adolescent males are more likely than any other demographic group to have a negative encounter with the police, and these negative encounters can have unfortunate consequences.[28] Given the police history of abuse, the dangerous culture, ethic, and the increasing tension with minority communities, I think it is fair to conclude that *the police have contributed to negative identities in African American adolescents and provoked oppositional responses.* This is not to lay the onus completely on the police or to fail to acknowledge the many officers who are truly peacekeepers at heart. When it comes to conflict, it takes two to tango. However, the focus of this book is on police reform; therefore the police need to reflect on how they have influenced this important demographic historically.

The historical conflicting identities underscore the need for the servant-shepherd officer. The servant-shepherd identity has the potential to project a positive model toward African American adolescents. The servant-shepherd officer is present and one with their people, treating all as intrinsically valuable and members of one united community. As a result, they are personal and actively engaged with their community while patrolling. The impact of the servant-shepherd identity in community-friendly encounters communicates a positive regard for all people, including African American adolescents.

As a protector, the servant-shepherd officer responds to help victims of crime and does not treat people in an impersonal way. The servant-shepherd officer has compassion for their people, and the care they provide strongly communicates a positive public regard. Furthermore, as a provider, they engage in activities and practices outside the norm, ensuring encounters with African American adolescents are not reduced to enforcement action only. Within their community, they purposefully and persistently build relationships and project an identity that communicates care, empathy, and respect, which helps African American adolescents have a positive regard for themselves. Since African American adolescents are at a critical formative period in identity formation, the servant-shepherd officer's actions are critical for promoting positive identities.

The servant-shepherd officer's active engagement in the community is fundamental and sets the stage for investigative stops. By laying a relational foundation, the servant-shepherd officer reduces the salience of investigative encounters with African American adolescents, making them more likely to have personally experienced or at least vicariously experienced a positive encounter with police.[29] As a result, the war of identities is less likely to be a catalyst for violence. Instead, salience is likely to be reduced because the identity of the servant-shepherd officer is not contentious. The encounter, therefore, is far less likely to cultivate hostility and aggression that ends in violence.

As a school resource officer, I had frequent friendly encounters with students for years. This type of interaction is simply part of the job. Some years later, I encountered a few of these former students in the streets under less-than-fortunate circumstances. There were times I arrived at the scene of an incident where a former student was in a volatile confrontation with officers that appeared to be progressing to where force would have to be used. When the person would see me, it was not uncommon for them to completely change their posture and comply. The change was not due to anything I did in the moment but because the mistrust and hostility was diffused by trust, and the trust was earned far before we came to the contentious moment at hand. This experience is surely not unique to me. Many school resource officers could testify to similar instances simply because when they return to the streets, they inevitably encounter people who have a different posture toward them due to the personal and positive interactions that took place years before in the school.

Likewise, through intentional social encounters, the servant-shepherd officer projects a positive outlook toward a people group promoting feelings of value and respect in African American adolescents, which sets the stage for future peaceful resolutions in turbulent circumstances. In short, *when police officers act as servant-shepherds, they can contribute to the development of positive identities in African American adolescents and promote peaceful interactions.*

Although this chapter has focused on the police and their contribution to the violent encounters taking place between law enforcement and African Americans, in no way am I suggesting that the police are the sole contributors to this problem or that they are singularly responsible for solving it. However, every police officer is a leader in the community. As a result, responsibility for change should start with leadership. The police, therefore, should focus on their contribution to the problem and how best to respond to promote peace in their communities.

Some in law enforcement may attribute the problem solely to the African American community, and some in the African American community may believe the police are the single contributing factor to the problem. Neither of these perspectives is accurate or helpful. Clearly, the investment in cultivating positive identities in African American youth is a long-term strategy, but there are no quick fixes here. The police need to embrace the reality that the persistence of confrontational and aggressive practices of the past has made an investment resulting in the current chaos. None of this came to be overnight, and it will not resolve itself without a vision for the long term.

WHAT IF WE DID SOMETHING BEFORE IT'S TOO LATE?

As a police officer, I have had to deliver death notifications on many occasions. Telling someone their loved one has died is never easy. I've seen sisters grieve over the loss of their siblings, children over the loss of their parents, and fathers over the loss of their children. Every person feels the pain of losing someone they loved, but from my experience, the grief a mother feels when her son or daughter dies is far deeper. I'll never forgot one such occasion.

A young man, who we will call Tim, lived with his mother in a low-income housing project. When Tim entered his teen years, he became unruly, and his mother desperately tried to get him back on track. As a single mother, she worked long hours at a fast-food restaurant. I do not remember a single time I spoke with her when she was not in her uniform. Tim was failing school and selling drugs, running the streets without coming home for days at a time. On different occasions, I would find him after his mother reported him missing, or I would be called to the house because he was behaving disrespectfully toward his mother. I arrested him a few times for minor incidents, and as an officer, I could see that the situation would not likely end well for him. I thought he would end up in prison.

When Tim turned eighteen, he continued with this behavior. Around that time, I was promoted and no longer regularly responded to common calls for service, so I lost touch with Tim and his mother. About seven years later, as a lieutenant, I responded to a murder at Tim's mother's residence. Arriving on scene, Tim lay dead just twenty feet from his mother's front door, gunned down in front of several witnesses. I knew we would have to tell Tim's mother, and I knew we would be delivering the most life-shattering news she had ever received. I called an African American pastor from the community to help provide comfort to Tim's mother. On learning the news, she crumpled into the pastor's arms, sobbing in inconsolable grief. The broken heart of a mother weeping for her child is unbearable to witness. I had to look away as her sobbing grieved my own soul. Even to this day, I can hear the echoes of the sobs of Tim's mother.

I attended Tim's funeral, and the church was filled with young African Americans, some of whom were living a similar lifestyle as the man we were memorializing. The pastor leading the service was a tall African American man in his sixties. He had a deep, commanding voice, but his tone revealed his immense grief and pain over Tim's death. I'll never forget his words to the crowd of young people: "I see you in church with your mothers, and everything seems fine. Then sometime—usually during junior high or high school—I don't see you anymore. Until . . ." With a strong upright posture, he gestured down to the casket with his giant open hands in utter grief and with tear-filled eyes.

I have found it difficult to motivate police officers toward interest in atypical police functions, like community-friendly activities that engage teens. A common response is, "We aren't social workers." Certainly, some officers are highly motivated to engage in these spaces, but doing so is countercultural. It's always the few.

A few officers with a different perspective can only make a limited difference. However, a department transformed by the servant-shepherd model and ethic that cultivates a culture of servanthood would produce servant-shepherd officers. For the servant-shepherd officer, these community functions would cease to be countercultural and instead become the norm. When these functions are no longer atypical, I believe we will see fewer mothers weeping over the premature deaths of their children. One less grieving mother is worth the investment, and it is far more valuable than arrest statistics.

CONCLUSION

When I was a rookie officer over twenty-five years ago, I was aware that while some people did not care for the police, others really valued us. As the years passed and especially in the later stages of my career, the gap between those two positions only grew. People who didn't care for us before grew to hate us, and those who appreciated us started making great efforts to express their thanks. I think my experience reflects the current political/social environment of today, where some want to abolish the police and others fiercely resist any notion that law enforcement needs reform. As I bring this book to a close, I hope it is clear that I am not calling for the abolition or de-funding of the police. Still, even as I realize that many of our officers are wonderful public servants, policing as a profession needs reform.

I believe that the Christian pastoral leadership theory I've laid out here—Christ-centered followership—has the po-tential to transform the culture of the police, which has con-tributed to the dangerous trend of social distance, dehuman-ization, and abuse. The police's oppositional relationship with the public is exacerbated by their current leadership structure and embedded utilitarian ethic, which manifests in an enforcement-centric mission and culminates in a systemi-cally racist strategy leading to confrontations that have often resulted in abuse.

The servant-shepherd leadership model can reverse this dangerous cultural trend by emphasizing a new relationship and ethic that focuses the police on a mission of peacekeeping. Pairing it with the procedural justice model of police legitimacy and community policing can provide the strategy needed to enable the servant-shepherd officer to promote harmony, peace, and human flourishing in racial minority communities. Figure 10.1 provides a juxtaposition of the current police context with a police context reformed by the servant-shepherd leadership model and ethic.

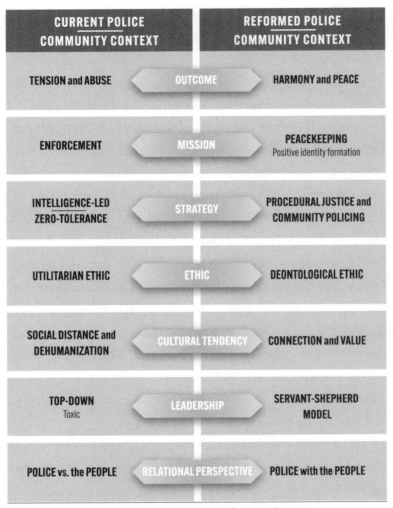

CURRENT POLICE COMMUNITY CONTEXT		REFORMED POLICE COMMUNITY CONTEXT
TENSION and ABUSE	OUTCOME	HARMONY and PEACE
ENFORCEMENT	MISSION	PEACEKEEPING Positive identity formation
INTELLIGENCE-LED ZERO-TOLERANCE	STRATEGY	PROCEDURAL JUSTICE and COMMUNITY POLICING
UTILITARIAN ETHIC	ETHIC	DEONTOLOGICAL ETHIC
SOCIAL DISTANCE and DEHUMANIZATION	CULTURAL TENDENCY	CONNECTION and VALUE
TOP-DOWN Toxic	LEADERSHIP	SERVANT-SHEPHERD MODEL
POLICE vs. the PEOPLE	RELATIONAL PERSPECTIVE	POLICE with the PEOPLE

Figure 10.1. Current police/community context versus reformed police/community context

Policing is a redeemable profession, and it remains full of men and women today who serve with honor and integrity. During my tenure, I witnessed amazing acts of sacrifice, valor, and charity. For example, toward the end of my career, my officers and I responded to a young African American man who had been shot in the thigh. He was bleeding profusely when we arrived. One of my officers, a White male, tied a tourniquet around the young man's leg without donning any protective equipment. The ambulance did not arrive until a few minutes later, and the officer's selfless act undoubtedly saved the young man's life.

As a police lieutenant, I was responsible for the safety of not only the public but also my officers. After the man was transported to the hospital, I pulled the officer aside and reminded him that he should have put on his gloves and protective equipment. He simply replied that if he had taken the time to do so, the young man may not have survived. This officer did not know the shooting victim. They were complete strangers, and he was well aware of the danger of blood-borne pathogens.

My time in law enforcement saw many powerful acts from the police. On one occasion, an officer and friend of mine plunged into near-freezing lake water to rescue a young lady who had driven her car off a pier to commit suicide. Another time, as Christmas approached, an officer I knew withdrew three hundred dollars from his own bank and gave it to a young African American woman with a disabled child who had no money to help them celebrate the holiday.

Yet, despite regular examples of integrity and honor across my department, I had known for years that there was a glaring problem in policing. The death of George Floyd was shocking and raised my concern to a greater level. If someone had told me an incident like that could have occurred prior to that day in Minneapolis, I would have denied the possibility. Certainly, I believed there were officers malicious enough to commit the act, but to do so knowing full well you are being recorded requires both maliciousness and utter stupidity. I believed this despicable combination was extremely unlikely to exist in one person. Clearly, I was wrong—I underestimated the formative power of police culture on the most depraved among us.

Although every officer I have encountered thus far renounces the officer's conduct and application of force against George Floyd, very few agree with my assessment of the police, particularly my view that our practices are systemically racist. But law enforcement officers must remember, I come from within. I am through and through one of them. My hope is that this reality keeps my voice from being so easily dismissed.

Police culture is only one aspect of a larger problem. Many officers point to other factors that contribute to the problem of police brutality, but I believe we should start with how we contribute to the problem, and perhaps leave it to others whose voices may best be heard by the community to address other contributing factors. While many still believe the aggressive police tactics of the past are what keep officers safe, watching the civil unrest unfold throughout this country, I vehemently disagree.

Relationship is what will protect the police and community. I learned this as a young officer surrounded in a crowd of three hundred African Americans who had flooded into the street after exiting a bar where fights had erupted. If that crowd had wanted to hurt me, there was nothing I could have done to prevent it. One other officer and I were surrounded by the crowd. We were completely at their mercy. They began to throw bottles at us, but as they did, two African American young men stepped out of the crowd and stood with us. They were two of my friends from high school, and their presence stopped the press of the crowd toward us. This is the power of community relations.

Of course, other factors contribute to police brutality, particularly cultural factors related to the community, but we need to rise above an either-or solution to the problem, one that says it is either due to systemic racism or it is due to cultural factors. An either-or position limits our potential to recognize the depth of the problem and offer real and workable solutions. Worth noting, this book argued for a cultural problem that has led to systemic racism. The two need not be mutually exclusive, as they are, perhaps, inextricably bound together.

The church is in the best position to address this problem in society, as it can speak to both cultural and systemically racist issues. What I mean by the church are both Christians in law enforcement and Christians in the community—one people. If we identified first as Christians, perhaps brothers and sisters from all occupations and races could shed the myopic assessment of the problem. Christians should be the frontrunners for integration, unity, and open-minded problem solving that transcends the socially constructed identities of a world and age that will come to an end in our Lord Jesus Christ.

NOTES

INTRODUCTION: AWAKENING TO CULTURAL BLINDNESS

[1]Frederick Douglass, *Narrative of the Life of Frederick Douglass, an American Slave* (New York: Barnes and Noble Classics, 2003), 26.

[2]Douglass, *Narrative of the Life*, 26.

[3]See Gina Robertiello, *The Use and Abuse of Police Power in America* (Santa Barbara, CA: ABC-CLIO, 2017).

[4]See Malcolm D. Holmes and Brad W. Smith, *Race and Police Brutality: Roots of an Urban Dilemma* (Albany: State University of New York Press, 2008).

[5]Robertiello, *The Use and Abuse of Police Power*, 221. Jeff Pegues references a 2013 survey in the *New York Times* that showed that only 32 percent of African Americans believed that police relations with African Americans have improved since 1963. Furthermore, in 2014, a year after Michael Brown was killed, the Pew Research Center conducted a survey, and 80 percent of African Americans surveyed believed the incident "raised important issues about race." Jeff Pegues, *Black and Blue: Inside the Divide Between the Police and Black America* (Amherst, NY: Prometheus Books, 2017), 101.

[6]Anthony Stanford, *Copping Out: The Consequences of Police Corruption and Misconduct* (Santa Barbara, CA: Praeger, 2015), 166.

[7]Myisha Cherry provides a unique understanding of rage in her book. Rage is described closely to a righteous indignation that becomes an impetus for actions that address racism and social injustice. See Myisha Cherry, *The Case for Rage* (New York: Oxford University Press, 2021).

[8]*Police brutality* refers to any excessive use of force by police when use of force is assessed in relation to the factors that warranted an arrest or seizure by the police and the reasonable use of force to counteract a person's resistance. See

Jeff Rojek, Scott H. Decker, and Allen E. Wagner, "Addressing Police Misconduct: The Role of Citizen Complaints," in *Critical Issues in Policing*, ed. Roger G. Dunham and Geoffrey P. Alpert, (Long Grove, IL: Waveland Press, 2015), 165.

[9]Robertiello, *The Use and Abuse of Police Power*, 66. Robertiello overviews the history of law enforcement reform by noting the key court decisions, federal commissions, and local law enforcement applications that were largely a result of controversial and abusive applications by local law enforcement. Many of the changes were orchestrated because of the police using force against African Americans. The Los Angeles "zoot suit riots" are an early example, and the beating of Rodney King is a more recent incident that led to organizational changes in local law enforcement.

[10]Holmes and Smith note, "The findings of various empirical studies support the argument that racial/ethnic minorities are victimized disproportionately by police brutality." Furthermore, the authors note that law enforcement agencies rely on organizational reforms implemented through training and supervision to reduce police brutality. Holmes and Smith, *Race and Police Brutality*, 9. However, Robertiello notes the "difficulty to change police behavior via training" related to police brutality given the current overarching philosophy of law enforcement. Robertiello, *The Use and Abuse of Police Power*, 205.

[11]Pegues notes, "According to a 2013 survey conducted just before the fiftieth anniversary of Martin Luther King, Jr.'s March on Washington, 48 percent of whites claimed that a lot of progress has been made since 1963, yet only 32 percent of blacks agreed with that assessment of police relations." Pegues, *Black and Blue*, 101.

[12]For the purposes of this research, "external factors" are factors related to departmental rules, policies, structures, and disciplinary measures, in addition to federal, state, and local laws that govern the police. See D. W. Stephens, "Organization in Management," in *Local Government Police Management*, 4th ed., ed. William A. Geller and Darrel W. Stephens (Wilmette, IL: ICMA Publishers, 2003), 47-48.

[13]I will thoroughly explain the specific court decisions and commissions and the phenomenon of resistance in later chapters.

[14]The working definition was drawn from Holmes and Smith, *Race and Police Brutality*, 25.

[15]See Barbara E. Armacost, "Organizational Culture and Police Misconduct," *The George Washington Law Review*, 72 (2003–2004), 453-56.

[16]Holmes and Smith explain that police officers have a formative subculture that results in a social identity. The social identity of police officers is disparate from the social identity of racial minorities. This disparity contributes to social distance and ultimately leads to a proclivity for abuse. Holmes and Smith, *Race and Police Brutality*, 52-53.

[17]The working definition was drawn from Holmes and Smith, *Race and Police Brutality*, 4-8.

[18]Daniel J. Daily notes that social structures influence moral agents, yet sinful people construct social structures in which sinful proclivities become embedded. This reciprocal relationship draws attention to the influence that such structures can have on an individual's actions. Daniel J. Daily, "Structures of Virtue and Vice," *New Blackfriars* 92 (2011): 341-57. Social structures are formed by a collective of individuals but have an independent existence and influence individuals that are part of the structure. Social structures have causal impact on individuals and exhibit norms that affect individuals within the structure. These norms are in the form of restrictions, enablements, and incentives. Daniel K. Finn, "What Is a Sinful Social Structure?" *Theological Studies* 77, no. 1 (2016): 136-64. Jack L. Colwell and Charles Huth note, "The [police] department member is allowed (if not encouraged) to entertain demeaning, prejudicial attitudes and have private conversations that are slanderous and defaming." Jack L. Colwell and Charles Huth, *Unleashing the Power of Unconditional Respect: Transforming Law Enforcement and Police Training* (New York: CRC Press, 2010), xvii.

[19]Philip Zimbardo attempts to answer why seemingly good people commit evil acts. He analyzes the Stanford prison experiment and proposes that there were systemic contributions to the phenomenon of evil actions. He notes that dehumanization, power, and systemic problems within culture are all contributing factors. Philip Zimbardo, *The Lucifer Effect: Understanding How Good People Turn Evil* (New York: Random House, 2008).

[20]For instance, Thomas Sowell in *Black Red Necks and White Liberals* explains racial disparity through culture. Conversely, Michelle Alexander in *The New Jim Crow* explains racial disparity through systemic racism.

[21]Armacost provides important insights into police organizational culture and how leadership and cultural change are necessary for any lasting reform. She wrote, "It follows that no legal strategy that ignores the power of the police organization will have any lasting success in addressing police brutality. . . . The only way that individual cops will change is if the organizational culture

changes, and the only way that organization will change is if high-level offi-
cials are held accountable for the actions of their subordinates." Armacost,
"Organizational Culture and Police Misconduct," 521.

²²See Thomas Sowell, *Discrimination and Disparities* (New York: Basic
Books, 2019).

²³Paula A. Braveman, Elaine Arkin, Dwayne Proctor, Tina Kauh, and Nicole Holm,
"Systemic and Structural Racism: Definitions, Examples, Health Damages, and
Approaches to Dismantling," *Health Affairs* 41, no. 2 (2022): 171.

²⁴Chapter one will explicate and detail the Christian presuppositions that
undergirded Robert Peel's formational principles for modern police
departments.

²⁵See H. Richard Niebuhr, *Christ and Culture* (New York: HarperCollins, 2001).

²⁶D. A. Carson is concerned with understanding the current relationship in
modern culture with Christ. He reviews Richard Niebuhr's five conceptions
of the relationship between Christ and culture. He still finds merit in
Niebuhr's work; however, Niebuhr conceived of culture too broadly and was
too inclusive of heretical movements within Christianity. As a result,
Niebuhr's five patterns need to be amended in light of a broader understanding of culture and essential biblical theology that excludes heresy.
Nonetheless, Niebuhr's five patterns are helpful when the shortcomings are
understood and when they are applied holistically by recognizing relevant
aspects of each pattern without resorting to categorical application.
Furthermore, Carson points out that culture cannot be seen as devoid of all
Christian identity, as Niebuhr postulated, because culture is constructed
historically from inherited concepts directed at a collective understanding
of life. Carson recognizes the tension in every culture as being against
Christ in some sense, yet simultaneously recognizes the mandate to
transform culture. As a result, he advocates reliance on Scripture as a guide
for thinking and action. D. A. Carson, *Christ and Culture Revisited* (Grand
Rapids, MI: Eerdmans, 2008).

1. A HISTORY OF THE POLICE

¹See Bryan Vila and Cynthia Morris, *The Role of Police in American Society*
(Westport, CT: Greenwood Press, 1999), xxxi.

²Pamela Mayhall lists Peel's principles: "1. The basic mission for which the
police exist is to prevent crime and disorder as an alternative to the repression of crime and disorder by military force and severity of legal punishment. 2. The ability of the police to perform their duties is dependent

upon public approval of police existence, actions, behavior and the ability of the police to secure and maintain public respect. 3. The police must secure the willing cooperation of the public in voluntary observance of the law to be able to secure and maintain public respect. 4. The degree of cooperation of the public that can be secured diminishes, proportionally, to the necessity for the use of physical force and compulsion in achieving police objectives. 5. The police seek and preserve public favor, not by catering to public opinion, but by constantly demonstrating absolutely impartial service to the law, in complete independence of policy, and without regard to the justice or injustice of the substance of individual laws; by ready offering of individual service and friendship to all members of society without regard to their race or social standing, by ready exercise of courtesy and good humor; and by ready offering of individual sacrifice in protecting and preserving life. 6. The police should use physical force to the extent necessary to secure observance of the law or to restore order only when the exercise of persuasion, advice and warning is found to be insufficient to achieve police objectives; and police should use only the minimum degree of physical force, which is necessary on any particular occasion for achieving a police objective. 7. The police at all times should maintain a relationship with the public that gives reality to the historic tradition that the police are the public and the public are the police; the police are the only members of the public who are paid to give fulltime attention to duties, which are incumbent on every citizen in the intent of the community welfare. 8. The police should always direct their actions toward their functions and never appear to usurp the powers of the judiciary by avenging individuals or the state, or authoritatively judging guilt or punishing the guilty. 9. The test of police efficiency is the absence of crime and disorder, not the visible evidence of police action in dealing with them." Pamela D. Mayhall, *Police-Community Relations and the Administration of Justice* (New York: John Wiley and Sons, 1985), 425-26.

[3]Sir Robert Peel, quoted in George Kelling, "The Evolution of Contemporary Policing," in *Local Government Police Management*, 4th ed., ed. William A. Geller and Darrel W. Stephens (Wilmette, IL: ICMA Publishers, 2003), 3.

[4]M. A. Lewis, "Peel's Legacy," *The FBI Law Enforcement Bulletin* 80, no. 12 (December 2011): 8. Eric J. Evans notes Peel's background in explaining his view of Roman Catholicism: "As an early-nineteenth-century Protestant, also, Peel's background and upbringing conditioned him to believe that

Roman Catholicism was a primitive, authoritarian religion appropriate only to simple minds and inimical to liberty and freedom of speech." Eric J. Evans, *Sir Robert Peel: Statesmanship, Power and Party*, 2nd ed. (New York: Routledge, 2006), 9. Lewis notes that Peel was sympathetic to "British evangelicals'" protests of the legal system, which contributed to Peel's "sweeping penal reform." Lewis, "Peel's Legacy," 8.

[5] Vila and Morris note, "Early attempts at more effective policing occurred on a small scale in Philadelphia in 1833 and in Boston in 1838, but it wasn't until 1845 that America's first unified, prevention-oriented police force was established in New York City . . . patterned after the London Metropolitan Police." Vila and Morris, *The Role of Police*, 35.

[6] Vila and Morris, *The Role of Police*, 35.

[7] Larry K. Gaines, Victor E. Kappeler, and Joseph B. Vaughn state that officers did not take enforcement action against brothels and gambling institutions if the owners were affiliated with the politicians in control of the police department. Furthermore, New York City had a going rate for promotions: "15,000 was the going rate for captain's positions . . . the police, in essence, served as the collection agents for political bosses. . . . In many respects, the political stranglehold on the police was total and consuming." Larry K. Gaines, Victor E. Kappeler, and Joseph B. Vaughn, *Policing in America*, 3rd ed. (Cincinnati: Anderson Publishing, 1999), 84-85.

[8] Gaines, Kappeler, and Vaughn, *Policing in America*, 83.

[9] Gina Robertiello, *The Use and Abuse of Police Power in America* (Santa Barbara, CA: ABC-CLIO, 2017), 57.

[10] Kelling explains, "Financial corruption and inequitable, discriminatory, inefficient, and brutal policing thrives. . . . Such characterizations of US police were to continue during at least the first two decades of the twentieth century. Indeed, if anything, police corruption worsened with the ratification of the Prohibition amendment to the Constitution in 1920." Kelling, "The Evolution of Contemporary Policing," 4.

[11] Kelling notes that August Volmer, "the father of modern policing," applied "scientific principles" to criminal investigation, promotions, and hiring practices. Kelling, "The Evolution of Contemporary Policing," 4.

[12] Kelling explains, "Managerial authority was being centralized in the office of the chief; command and control concepts . . . were being implemented to rationalize police departments." Kelling, "The Evolution of Contemporary Policing," 6.

[13]Gaines, Kappeler, and Vaughn note, "Many administrators felt that automobile patrol made officers less accessible to the public. . . . In the past, the foot patrol officer was viewed as part of the neighborhood, a resource for citizens to turn to in time of trouble. In essence, the officer was more a community adviser and helper than a law enforcement agent." Gaines, Kappeler, and Vaughn, *Policing in America*, 199.

[14]Gaines, Kappeler, and Vaughn, *Policing in America*, 91.

[15]Kelling explains, "Indeed, with rare exception police defined themselves as *professional* organizations that should be kept out of the purview of citizens, academics, and researchers, and other persons with an interest in police. Police business was just that: *police* business." Kelling, "The Evolution of Contemporary Policing," 10.

[16]Kelling writes, "When African Americans rioted in many cities during the 1960s . . . postmortems noted long-festering tensions between mostly white police departments and minority-group neighborhoods." Kelling, "The Evolution of Contemporary Policing," 12.

[17]Robertiello notes, "Police departments across America were experiencing the repercussions of the movement toward professionalism. . . . The goal was to essentially isolate police from the community in an effort to protect officers from temptations. . . . The danger of this approach, however, was that in many municipalities, the police became so detached from the communities . . . that they were increasingly viewed as outsiders." Robertiello, *The Use and Abuse of Police Power*, 98-99.

[18]Gaines, Kappeler, and Vaughn note, "During the 1960s, the civil rights movement intensified. This, combined with feelings of impoverishment and helplessness in the ghettos, created civil unrest. Almost every major city in the United States had a major riot between 1964 and 1968." Gaines, Kappeler, and Vaughn, *Policing in America*, 92.

[19]Gaines, Kappeler, and Vaughn reference the turbulent political climate of the 1960s and specifically the multiple assassinations and conclude, "It became evident that the police were not prepared for or capable of dealing with the civil strife that occurred in the 1960s." Gaines, Kappeler, and Vaughn, *Policing in America*, 93. Craig D. Uchida explains, "Policing in America encountered its most serious crisis in the 1960s. The rise in crime, the civil rights movement, anti-war sentiment, and riots in the cities brought the police into the center of a maelstrom." Craig D. Uchida, "The Development of the American Police: An Historical Overview," in *Critical*

Issues in Policing, 7th ed., ed. Roger G. Dunham and Geoffrey P. Alpert (Long Grove, IL: Waveland Press, 2015), 23.

[20]Kelling references demonstrations and riots as well as court actions and crime commissions in support of his categorization of the 1960s as a time of "shocks and change." Kelling, "The Evolution of Contemporary Policing," 12-15.

[21]Charles R. Swanson, Leonard Territo, and Robert W. Taylor note, "34 people were killed . . . and losses amounted to $200 million" in Watts. Furthermore, "similar riots struck more than two dozen major cities." Charles R. Swanson, Leonard Territo, and Robert W. Taylor, *Police Administration: Structures, Processes, and Behaviors*, 8th ed. (Upper Saddle River, NJ: Pearson, 2012), 17.

[22]Robertiello describes the event as receiving "vivid media coverage of the clashes between police and demonstrators.' Robertiello, *The Use and Abuse of Police Power*, 102.

[23]Vila and Morris, *The Role of Police*, 183.

[24]Robertiello notes, "The commission was directed to answer three questions related to the summer of 1967 that saw racial disorders, such as protests and riots, across the United States: (1) What happened? (2) Why did it happen? and (3) What can be done to prevent it from happening again?" Robertiello, *The Use and Abuse of Police Power*, 95.

[25]Vila and Morris, *The Role of Police*, 190.

[26]Vila and Morris quote the commission: "We have cited deep hostility between the police and ghetto communities as a primary cause of disorders surveyed by the Commission. In Newark, Detroit, Watts, and Harlem—in practically every city that has experienced racial disruption since the summer of 1964—abrasive relationships between police and Negroes and other minority groups have been a major source grievance, tension and, ultimately, disorder." Vila and Morris, *The Role of Police*, 190.

[27]Kelling explains, "1961: Evidence illegally seized by police cannot be used against state-level criminal defendants (*Mapp v. Ohio*). . . . 1966: Suspects have the right to counsel when criminal investigations begin to focus on them; they must be informed of their right to remain silent (*Miranda v. Arizona*)." Kelling, "The Evolution of Contemporary Policing," 12.

[28]Vila and Morris note, "The Court's ruling established for the first time the legal right of the police to stop, question, and frisk a person who is behaving suspiciously, as long as the police officer has reasonable grounds for

perceiving the person's behavior as suspicious." Vila and Morris, *The Role of Police*, 187.

[29]Michael D. Coomes explains, "The Intercollegiate Socialist Society (ISS), an early radical organization, was founded in 1905. Numerous other student organizations . . . were founded in the 1920s, 1930 [sic], and 1940s. From the 1920s to the 1940s, these student groups confronted the impersonal nature of the rapidly growing higher education system, U.S. participation in both the First and Second World Wars, and advocated for international disarmament." Michael D. Coomes, "Students Armed with a Dream: The 1960s' New Left Student Movement," *Journal of College Student Development* 57, no. 3 (2016): 335.

[30]Coomes writes, "These issues would be echoed in the 1960s as college students in the New Left focused their energies on segregation, the war in Southeast Asia, the draft, U.S. imperialism, and authoritarian university structures." Coomes, "Students Armed with a Dream," 35.

[31]Herbert Marcuse explains, "The conclusion reached is that the realization of the objective of tolerance would call for intolerance toward prevailing policies, attitudes, opinions, and the extension of tolerance to policies, attitudes, and opinions which are outlawed or suppressed. In other words, today tolerance appears again as what it was in its origins, at the beginning of the modern period—a partisan goal, a subversive liberating notion and practice. Conversely, what is proclaimed and practiced as tolerance today, is in many of its most effective manifestations serving the cause of oppression. The author is fully aware that, at present, no power, no authority, no government exists which would translate liberating tolerance into practice, but he believes that it is the task and duty of the intellectual to recall and preserve historical possibilities which seem to have become utopian possibilities— that it is his task to break the concreteness of oppression in order to open the mental space in which this society can be recognized as what it is and does." Herbert Marcuse, "Repressive Tolerance," in *Critique of Pure Tolerance*, ed. Robert Paul Wolf, Barrington Moore, Jr., and Herbert Marcuse (Boston: Beacon Press, 1965), 82-83.

[32]H. J. G. Zandman notes, "The 1960s was a time of revolution. Young people were breaking out of the molds that were cast by their parents' post war era." H. J. G. Zandman, "The 1960s—Long Hair, Flowers and Morality Mash: Ethical Appraisal of the Clash That Helped Shape Today's Western Society," *In die Skriflig* 43, no. 1 (2009): 80. Jeffrey C. Alexander notes, "During the

sixties, the social unconscious reached up and grabbed us by our collective throat. It shook us violently and turned our world upside down. Our parents had deceived us, our teachers were oppressors, our political leaders criminals, our criminals saints. The old world was dying; a new one was being born." Jeffrey C. Alexander, "The Sixties and Me: From Cultural Revolution to Cultural Theory," *Revista Mexicana de Ciencias Politicas y Sociales* 63, no. 234 (2018): 101-102.

[33]Zandman notes, "The impartial observer cannot escape the irony of this peacekeeping generation's means to achieve its ends: violent expression and public disturbance often accompany their strive." Zandman, "The 1960s," 84.

[34]Vila and Morris quote the Kerner Commission: "In many ways, the policeman only symbolizes deeper problems. The policeman in the ghetto is a symbol not only of law, but of the entire system of law enforcement and criminal justice. As such, he becomes the tangible target of grievances against shortcomings throughout that system." Vila and Morris, *The Role of Police*, 190.

[35]Uchida notes, "The events of the 1960s forced the police, politicians, and policy makers to reassess the state of law enforcement in the United States. For the first time, academics rushed to study the police in an effort to explain their problems and crisis." Uchida, "The Development of the American Police," 25.

[36]Swanson, Territo, and Taylor reference specific research from the 1970s and conclude that the experiments "introduced new structure and processes and set the stage for other evolutionary police delivery concepts, such as community policing." Swanson, Territo, and Taylor, *Police Administration*, 21.

[37]Kelling references the work of Herman Goldstein, which argued for the implementation of problem-oriented policing, where the police focus efforts on problems that are the cause of crime and disorder. Additionally, the author references research arguing for cooperative efforts between the police and the community to reduce crime. Kelling, "The Evolution of Contemporary Policing," 19.

[38]For a basic understanding of the enforcement-centric strategy, intelligence-led policing, see Erik Fritzvold, "What Law Enforcement Leaders Should Know About Intelligence-Led Policing (ILP)," University of San Diego, accessed April 4, 2023, https://onlinedegrees.sandiego.edu/what-is-intelligence-led-policing.

[39]Jerome H. Skolnick and James J. Fyfe note that King was struck with a Taser and struck with batons fifty-six times. Furthermore, they note how the video tape allowed people "to see with their own eyes how a group of Los Angeles police officers could act in anger, frustration, fears, and prejudices on the body of a black man that led them on a high-speed chase." Jerome H. Skolnick and James J. Fyfe, *Above the Law: Police and the Excessive Use of Force* (New York: Free Press, 1993), 2-3.

[40]Robertiello notes, "The work of the Christopher Commission was a starting point for a broader movement relating to police reform and monitoring the quality of police-community relations. The Commission's work served as a model framework for hundreds of subsequent police department investigations and evaluations in the 20th and 21st centuries. As a result of such commissions, national efforts to address police-community relations and excessive use of force have been created." Robertiello, *The Use and Abuse of Police Power*, 189.

[41]Robertiello, *The Use and Abuse of Police Power*, 195.

[42]Robertiello explains, "This shooting sparked several protests, led by Reverend Al Sharpton and the National Action Network." Robertiello, *The Use and Abuse of Police Power*, 243.

[43]Robertiello writes, "The 2010s have witnessed an increased criminalization of public demonstrations. Additionally, the upsurge of police brutality has once again become more prevalent within the decade. More importantly, due to the rise of social media activism, many of these accounts of police abuse have been documented and posted on social media outlets, online newspapers, blogs, and YouTube. The Occupy Wall Street and Black Lives Matter movements are undoubtedly two of the largest social movements of the 21st century. These political and social demonstrations propelled into national movements making news headlines across the world." Robertiello, *The Use and Abuse of Police Power*, 221.

[44]Michael Ruth notes, "American police experienced a chaotic period in the mid-2010s. Multiple incidents across the United States in 2014 and 2015 left several African Americans dead at the hands of white police officers. In most cases, these deaths sparked violent protests. . . . Rioters claimed that police brutality and racism were overtaking the United States." Michael Ruth, *Police Brutality* (Farmington Hills, MI: Greenhaven, 2016), 19.

[45]Robertiello, *The Use and Abuse of Police Power*, 258-301. The author details the cases related to Brown, Garner, Ford, Rice, and Gray.

2. POLICE CULTURE

[1]Blue Lives Matter, "About Us," accessed March 30, 2023, https://archive
.bluelivesmatter.blue/organization/#history.

[2]Daniel K. Finn, "What Is a Sinful Social Structure?" *Theological Studies* 77,
no. 1 (2016): 151.

[3]Finn notes, "Social structures emerge from the activity of individuals, yet
have independent causal impact on people through the way social structures
affect (free but constrained) choices persons make." Finn, "What Is a Sinful
Social Structure?," 138.

[4]Finn explains, "And social structures have causal impact in the lives of those
persons through . . . the restrictions, enablement, and incentives which
structures present to individuals who operate within them. . . . The causal
impact occurs only because conscious human persons make decisions in light
of those restrictions, enablement, and incentives—decisions that might be
quite different had this person been facing different restrictions, enablement,
or incentives." Finn, "What Is a Sinful Social Structure?," 151.

[5]Daniel J. Daily references Vatican II and notes, "The council clearly maintained that social order profoundly influenced moral agents, for better and
for ill." Daniel J. Daily, "Structures of Virtue and Vice," *New Blackfriars* 92
(2011): 343. Additionally, Daily references the writings of Pope John Paul II
and states, "In keeping with previous papal statements, the passage showed
an awareness of the role of social structures in forming the consciences of
individual agents. The pope maintained that the individual conscience could
not be understood when abstracted from the society's conscience." Daily,
"Structures of Virtue and Vice," 350.

[6]Jerome H. Skolnick and James J. Fyfe, *Above the Law: Police and the Excessive
Use of Force* (New York: Free Press, 1993), 91.

[7]Joycelyn M. Pollock writes, "Many authors present versions of an informal
code of conduct that new officers are taught through informal socialization
that is quite different from the formal code of ethics. . . . What is obvious is
that the informal code of behavior . . . is different from the formal principles
as espoused by management." Joycelyn M. Pollock, *Ethical Dilemmas and
Decisions in Criminal Justice* (Belmont, CA: Cengage Learning, 2010), 116.

[8]Skolnick and Fyfe note, "The written rule is clear: cops are to use no more
force than necessary to subdue a suspect. Where a department subculture
condoning brutality prevails, the unwritten rule is: Teach them a lesson.'"
Skolnick and Fyfe, *Above the Law*, 13. Skolnick and Fyfe also write, "Police

also live by a profusion of such unwritten rules. Some have been adopted by police all over the Western world, such as customary ways of dealing with people who challenge police authority. Others are the unwritten norms prevailing in s specific department. Every police department has such written and unwritten guidelines, including the proprieties of accepting gratuities, discounts, bribes, and favors." Skolnick and Fyfe, *Above the Law*, 90.

[9]Malcolm D. Holmes and Brad W. Smith explain, "Informal norms and policies frequently outweigh the departmental regulations and statutory codes that govern policing. These unofficial procedures are passed to new recruits through informal socialization on the job, not during the formal training of the police academy. Above all, the police subculture reflects a shared group interests of those responsible for protecting society from wrongdoers. It is the existence of a powerful subculture which norms that form without reference to external constituencies or departmental policies that affirms the importance of understanding the street level actions of officers as reflections of the unique circumstances they confront on the job. While other factors influence their behavior, the normal formative framework for action is located in the subculture." Malcolm D. Holmes and Brad W. Smith, *Race and Police Brutality: Roots of an Urban Dilemma* (Albany: State University of New York Press, 2008), 25.

[10]I entered the field training program in 1998 after completing the police academy. It took place over four months and involved five veteran officers as field training officers. One of the training officers explained that the policy manual prescribed certain actions, but he would explain how it is really done on the street. Another field training officer advised us to forget everything we learned in the police academy and be ready to learn how it is really done. And still another training officer taught to "work backwards." By this he meant stopping people on the street without lawful reason, searching them, and once illegal contraband or any other arrestable offense was found, to type the report in a manner that justified the original stop. These guidelines and practices were considered the norm despite contradicting academy training, department policy, and the law.

[11]Holmes and Smith, *Race and Police Brutality*, 45. Additionally, Jeff Pegues interviewed a criminologist who responded to the root problems of police misconduct, noting that "a lot of [police misconduct] has to do with the police subculture where it becomes us-versus-them." Jeff Pegues, *Black and Blue: Inside the Divide Between the Police and Black America* (Amherst, NY: Prometheus Books, 2017), 125.

[12]Victor E. Kappeler, Richard D. Sluder, and Geoffrey P. Alpert note, "Isolation is an emotional and physical condition that makes it difficult for members of one social group to have relations and interact with members of another group. This feeling of separateness from the surrounding society is a frequently noted attribute of the police subculture in the United States. . . . Social isolation, as a theme of police subculture, is a logical result of the interaction of the police worldview and ethos of secrecy. Persons outside the police subculture are viewed somewhat warily as potential threats to the members' physical or emotional well-being, as well as to the officer's authority and autonomy." Victor E. Kappeler, Richard D. Sluder, and Geoffrey P. Alpert, "Breeding Deviant Conformity: The Ideology and Culture of Police," in *Critical Issues in Policing*, 7th ed., ed. Roger G. Dunham and Geoffrey P. Alpert (Long Grove, IL: Waveland Press, 2015), 92.

[13]Nicholas K. Peart notes, "[In 2010] the N.Y.P.D. recorded more than 600,000 stops; 84 percent of those stopped were blacks or Latinos." Nicholas K. Peart, "Why Is the N.Y.P.D. After Me?" *New York Times*, December 17, 2011. Hubert G. Locke references several studies and concludes, "What every study of police use of fatal force has found is that persons of color (principally Black males) are a disproportionately high percentage of the persons shot by the police." Hubert G. Locke, "The Color of Law and the Issue of Color: Race and the Abuse of Police Power," in *Police Violence*, ed. William A. Geller and Hans Toch (New Haven, CT: Yale University Press, 1996), 135.

[14]Locke notes several studies that illustrated "flunking the attitude test" or "contempt of cop" was a "significant factor in the police use of force." Locke, "The Color of Law and the Issue of Color," 143.

[15]Holmes and Smith note, "Citizens living in [minority neighborhoods] are caught in a double bind that is not of their making. While they may call upon the police to resolve the crimes and problems of disorder and fear, the arrival of the police may inject new threats into the situation and amplify the fear. A deep-seated fear of the police is prevalent among minorities." Holmes and Smith, *Race and Police Brutality*, 93. Pegues asserts that a "common denominator" related to communities where the police have shot a citizen "is a lack of trust between the police and the community." Pegues, *Black and Blue*, 120.

[16]Holmes and Smith note that difficult encounters with racial minorities cause the police to stereotype entire populations as "inherently dangerous" and "predisposes the police to suspicion and hostility." Holmes and Smith, *Race and Police Brutality*, 73.

[17]Kappeler, Sluder, and Alpert note that the "vast majority" of police officers are "middle-class white males." Furthermore, the authors note that in "2010, more than 75% of cities had had a police presence that was disproportionally white relative to the local population." Kappeler, Sluder, and Alpert, "Breeding Deviant Conformity," 84. They also note that, for instance, "black police officers are underrepresented in 72% of the communities where blacks comprise at least 5% of the population Hispanics are underrepresented in 66% of the cities where they make up at least 5% of the population." Kappeler, Sluder, and Alpert, "Breeding Deviant Conformity," 84.

[18]Skolnick and Fyfe assert, "America is, culturally speaking, two countries. One is urban, cosmopolitan, and multicultural. It suffers disproportionately from crime, gang violence, poverty, and homelessness. The other is suburban, relatively safe, relatively prosperous, and—most important—unicultural." Skolnick and Fyfe, *Above the Law*, xi. Gina Robertiello notes the divide in America that existed primarily between the opinions of middle-class White America and racial minorities in America concerning the death of Trayvon Martin and the issue of racial profiling: "The death of Trayvon Martin highlighted the ongoing and polarizing debate about causes and consequences of racial profiling. One side sees intentional discrimination and targeting as the biggest contributor to lethal violence, while the other side sees violence as a product of real threats, not intentional profiling, posed by violent criminals." Gina Robertiello, *The Use and Abuse of Police Power in America* (Santa Barbara, CA: ABC-CLIO, 2017), 254. Kappeler, Sluder, and Alpert note the hiring practices in law enforcement have led to a disproportionate number of middle-class White male officers that "are unable to identify with groups on the margins of traditional society." Kappeler, Sluder, and Alpert, "Breeding Deviant Conformity," 84.

[19]Jack L. Colwell and Charles Huth, *Unleashing the Power of Unconditional Respect: Transforming Law Enforcement and Police Training* (New York: CRC Press, 2010), 46.

[20]Colin Brown identifies elements of humanism: "(1) Man is not depraved; (2) the end of life is life itself, the good life on earth instead of the beatific life after death; (3) man is capable, guided solely by the light of reason and experience, of perfecting the good life on earth." Colin Brown, *Philosophy and the Christian Faith* (Downers Grove, IL: InterVarsity Press, 1968), 227. Paul Formosa supports Immanuel Kant's argument that the "human nature is radically evil," and concludes that Kant's theory "paints an eminently plausible picture of the human moral condition." Paul Formosa, "Kant on the

Radical Evil of Human Nature," *Philosophical Forum* (2007): 221. Stephen J. Duffy rejects the verity of the creation account in Genesis as well as the Christian concept of original sin in Genesis 3. However, he argues from a scientific perspective that there is biological, psychological, ontological, and sociological support "that deep within human beings there inheres a proclivity for evil." Stephen J. Duffy, "Genes, Original Sin and the Human Proclivity for Evil," *Horizons* 32, no. 2 (2005): 210-34. R. C. Sproul notes the Christian doctrine of original sin depicted in Genesis 3 and supported in the New Testament supports the human proclivity toward evil: "In Romans, Paul affirms that all mankind is naturally under the guilt and power of sin. . . . He traces this back to the sin of one man Adam. . . . It may be fairly claimed that the Fall narrative alone gives any convincing explanation of the perversity of human nature. Pascal said that the doctrine of original sin seems an offense to reason, but once accepted it makes total sense of the human condition. He was right; and the same thing may and should be said of the Fall narrative itself." R. C. Sproul, "The Fall," in *The Reformation Study Bible* (Orlando, FL: Ligonier Ministries, 2005), 13.

[21]Frederick Douglass, *The Narrative of the Life of Frederick Douglass, an American Slave* (New York: Barnes and Noble, 2003), 40.

[22]The Stanford prison experiment, although problematic in some respects, illustrates the behavior change that can take place when group identities exist and one group has power over another. The study may reflect the human proclivity for the abuse of power. The authors selected seemingly peaceful and well-adjusted college students to participate in a mock prison experiment. They randomly chose students to play the roles of guards and prisoners. The experiment quickly became problematic and behaviors changed dramatically. Craig Haney, Curtis Banks, and Philip Zimbardo, "Interpersonal Dynamics in a Simulated Prison," *Journal of Criminology and Penology* 1 (February 1973): 69-97.

[23]Michael J. Palmiotto notes that the States Civil Rights Commission stated, "Police officers possess awesome powers." Michael J. Palmiotto, *Police Use of Force: Important Issues Facing the Police and the Communities They Serve* (New York: CRC Press, 2017), 13.

[24]Philip Zimbardo, *The Lucifer Effect: Understanding How Good People Turn Evil* (New York: Random House, 2008), 307.

[25]Colwell and Huth postulate that officers dehumanize people and are able to justify their behavior: "When one person treats another as a 'less than

human object,' the human mind has an automatic proclivity to self-justify." Colwell and Huth, *Unleashing the Power of Unconditional Respect*, 16.

[26]See James K. A. Smith, *Desiring the Kingdom* (Grand Rapids, MI: Baker Academic, 2009).

3. TOXIC LEADERSHIP AND THE HIERARCHY OF POWER

[1]One unfortunate lieutenant angered a captain. The next day, he was reassigned and moved to a closet in the booking room. When you opened the door to the small, windowless room, the door struck his desk.

[2]Peter Northouse, *Leadership: Theory and Practice*, 8th ed. (Thousand Oaks, CA: Sage, 2019), 2-4.

[3]Bernard M. Bass and Ruth Bass explain, "In the first several decades of the twentieth century, leadership was a matter of impressing the will of the leader and inducing obedience. Currently, in the age of information, leadership is seen more as consulting and shared decision making." Bernard M. Bass and Ruth Bass, *The Bass Handbook of Leadership: Theory, Research, & Managerial Applications*, 4th ed. (New York: Free Press, 2008), 24.

[4]Bass and Bass write, "The more recent definitions conceive of leadership in terms of influence relationships, power differentials, persuasion, influence on goal achievement, role differentiation, reinforcement, initiation of structure, and perceived attributions of behavior that are consistent with what the perceivers believe leadership to be." Bass and Bass, *The Bass Handbook of Leadership*, 24.

[5]Bass and Bass explain, "Authority is the legitimate right to exercise power, but it depends on the willingness of others to accept it. . . . Authority is both allocated from above and acknowledged from below before it converts into power." Bass and Bass, *The Bass Handbook of Leadership*, 365.

[6]Bass and Bass write that authority from above "is less often the main source of leadership than it used to be." Bass and Bass, *The Bass Handbook of Leadership*, 365.

[7]Gary Yukl and Nishant Uppal explain, "Position power includes potential influence derived from legitimate authority, control over resources and rewards, control over punishments, control over information, and control over the physical work environment." Gary Yukl and Nishant Uppal, *Leadership in Organizations*, 8th ed. (Tamil Nadu, India: Pearson, 2013), 209.

[8]Yukl and Uppal, *Leadership in Organizations*, 206.

[9]Yukl and Uppal write, "Over the last two centuries, there has been a general decline in use of legitimate coercion by all types of leaders. For

example, most managers once had the right to dismiss employees for any reason they thought justified. The captain of a ship could flog sailors who were disobedient or who failed to perform their duties diligently. Military officers could execute a soldier for desertion or failure to obey an order during combat. Nowadays, these forms of coercive power are prohibited or sharply restricted in many nations." Yukl and Uppal, *Leadership in Organizations*, 206.

[10]Northouse notes, "Our definition of leadership stresses *using influence* to bring individuals toward a common goal, while coercion involves the use of threats and punishment to *induce change* in followers for the sake of leaders. Coercion runs counter to leadership because it does not treat leadership as a process that emphasizes working *with* followers to achieve objectives." Northouse, *Leadership*, 15-16.

[11]Yukl and Uppal, *Leadership in Organizations*, 232.

[12]Yukl and Uppal, *Leadership in Organizations*, 206.

[13]Barbara Kellerman posits, "Leadership has a long history and a clear trajectory. More than anything else it is about the devolution of power—from those up top to those down below." Barbara Kellerman, *The End of Leadership* (New York: HarperCollins, 2012), 3. She also writes, "In the last one hundred years, relations between leaders and followers reached a turning point, if not a tipping point. Leader power and follower power became more equivalent." Kellerman, *The End of Leadership*, 16. Kellerman continues, "Followers on the rise, leaders in decline—while the trend could be traced back over hundreds of years, in the 1960s and '70s it accelerated, again particularly in the United States." Kellerman, *The End of Leadership*, 20.

[14]Bass and Bass note, "The past century saw a rise and acceleration of a movement to change the distribution of power by delegating decision making to lower levels of organizational management and employees closer to the need for action. Power sharing took on a life of its own as empowerment at all organizational levels became a popular strategy in the 1980s." Bass and Bass, *The Bass Handbook of Leadership*, 304.

[15]Bass and Bass, *The Bass Handbook of Leadership*, 318.

[16]Brigitte Steinheider and Todd Wuestewald affirm, "Contemporary policing has moved from reactive to proactive strategies, such as community policing (COP) and intelligence-led policing. The focus has shifted from leadership at the top to leadership at the bottom, where the discretionary activities of front line officers can make a real difference in terms of community

engagement, prevention, and interdiction. However, modern police organizations remain largely centralized in their decision-making, structurally vertical, rule bound, and mired in power relationships." Brigitte Steinheider and Todd Wuestewald, "From the Bottom-Up: Sharing Leadership in a Police Agency," *Police Practice and Research* 9, no. 2 (May 2008): 145.

[17]Edward R. Maguire writes, "Police historians have shown that throughout the twentieth century, large municipal police organizations have become taller, more specialized, more formalized, and have devoted an increasing proportion of personnel to administrative functions. . . . As police organizations grow older, their personnel become less reliant on impersonal modes of supervisory control, and they develop more elaborated chains-of-command, formalized operations, and larger administrative staffs. . . . Older police organizations have more complex command structures because they have a longer history of adding new divisions and units, adding new levels of command, adding new formal rules and policies, and enlarging their administrative components." Edward R. Maguire, *Organizational Structure in American Police Agencies: Context, Complexity, and Control* (Albany: State University of New York Press, 2003), 78-79.

[18]Gary W. Cordner explains, "In a properly organized police department, the chief delegates authority for decision making to people at all levels within the organization. Authority is the power to make decisions or to perform tasks. The ultimate authority in a police department lies with the chief, who must wisely and widely delegate authority to others so that decisions can be made and tasks performed." Gary W. Cordner, *Police Administration*, 9th ed. (New York: Routledge, 2016), 112.

[19]Cordner notes, "Just as the chief has total authority over the entire police department, officers in high-ranking positions have more authority than those in lower ranks." Cordner, *Police Administration*, 113.

[20]Alicia L. Jurek, Mathew C. Matusiak, and Randa Embry Matusiak explain that current research suggests that the bureaucratic structure of police departments, as it grows more complex, results in increasing the social distance between ranks. Alicia L. Jurek, Mathew C. Matusiak, and Randa Embry Matusiak, "Structural Elaboration in Police Organizations: An Exploration," *Policing* 40, no. 2 (2017): 351.

[21]Michael J. Palmiotto addresses the danger of military rank structure: "Enhanced and inflated status has little to do with carrying out law enforcement functions. Instead, it can lead to a self-fulfilling prophecy whereby the chief

or high sheriff comes to believe they are, in fact, far superior to their fellow officers." Michael J. Palmiotto, *Police Use of Force: Important Issues Facing the Police and the Communities They Serve* (New York: CRC Press, 2017), 77.

22 Joris Lammers and Diederik A. Stapel argue that leaders with power increasingly dehumanize subordinates as a natural process to enable them to make difficult decisions: "Possession of power increases dehumanization." Joris Lammers and Diederik A. Stapel, "Power Increases Dehumanization," *Group Processes and Intergroup Relationships* 14, no. 1 (2011): 133.

23 Jack L. Colwell and Charles Huth note the bidirectionality of the us-versus-them mentality in law enforcement. They conclude that the "workplace cultures that are riddled with non-supervisory employees, who display an 'us versus them' mentality toward administrators, do not occur by accident." Jack L. Colwell and Charles Huth, *Unleashing the Power of Unconditional Respect: Transforming Law Enforcement and Police Training* (New York: CRC Press, 2010), 45. Jerome H. Skolnick and James J. Fyfe describe the social distance or "isolation" in police departments as "cops against bosses." Jerome H. Skolnick and James J. Fyfe, *Above the Law: Police and the Excessive Use of Force* (New York: Free Press, 1993), 122.

24 Steven R. Watt, Mitch Javidi, and Anthony H. Normore note facets of abusive leadership: "Coercion and intimidation as a leadership style; unprofessional behaviors such as unethical actions, discrimination, harassment, vulgarity, profanity, and rumor-mongering." Steven R. Watt, Mitch Javidi, and Anthony H. Normore, "Identifying and Combating Organizational Toxicity," *The Journal of California Law Enforcement* 49, no. 2 (2015): 21.

25 Robin Shepard Engel affirms that research supports "that style or quality of supervision can significantly influence patrol officer behavior." Robin Shepard Engel, "How Police Supervisory Styles Influence Patrol Behavior," in *Critical Issues in Policing*, 7th ed., ed. Roger G. Dunham and Geoffrey P. Alpert (Long Grove, IL: Waveland Press, 2015), 219.

26 Sean T. Hannah et al. sampled 2,572 military members and found that "abusive supervision may undermine moral agency." Sean T. Hannah et al., "Joint Influences of Individual and Work Unit Abusive Supervision on Ethical Intentions and Behaviors: A Moderated Mediation Model," *Journal of Applied Psychology* 98, no. 4 (2013): 579. Subsequently, they argued, "Abusive supervision can undermine followers' moral courage." Hannah et al., "Joint Influences," 581.

[27]Colwell and Huth, *Unleashing the Power of Unconditional Respect*, 11-12.

[28]There are of course exceptions to this, and officers are not to blindly follow orders. For instance, they should not concede to an unethical order. Nonetheless, officers must hold to their commitment to follow the orders given to them without delay or debate in most instances.

[29]Charles R. Swanson, Leonard Territo, and Robert W. Taylor explain, "The bureaucratic model is going to remain overwhelmingly the dominant type of structure. This does not mean that police administrators should ignore or fail to try to reduce dysfunctional aspects of the bureaucracy; rather reform efforts will generally take the form of improvements in how the bureaucratic model operates and is experienced by both employees and clients as opposed to abandoning it altogether." Charles R. Swanson, Leonard Territo, and Robert W. Taylor, *Police Administration: Structures, Processes, and Behaviors*, 8th ed. (Upper Saddle River, NJ: Pearson, 2012), 210.

4. BIAS AND BRUTALITY

[1]Joycelyn M. Pollock, *Ethical Dilemmas and Decisions in Criminal Justice*, 7th ed. (Belmont, CA: Cengage Learning, 2012), 30.

[2]Cyndi Banks, *Criminal Justice Ethics: Theory and Practice*, 5th ed. (Thousand Oaks, CA: Sage, 2020), 26.

[3]Graham v. Ohio, 490 U.S. 386 (1989).

[4]Jonathan Blanks, "Thin Blue Lies: Pretextual Stops Undermine Police Legitimacy," *Case Western Reserve Law Review* 66, no. 4 (2016): 932.

[5]Michelle Alexander poses the same question. See Michelle Alexander, *The New Jim Crow: Mass Incarceration in an Age of Colorblindness* (New York: New Press, 2010).

[6]Jerry H. Ratcliffe provides a succinct definition: "Intelligence-led policing emphasises analysis and intelligence as pivotal to an objective, decision-making framework that prioritises crime hot spots, repeat victims, prolific offenders and criminal groups. It facilitates crime and harm reduction, disruption and prevention through strategic and tactical management, deployment, and enforcement." Jerry H. Ratcliffe, *Intelligence-Led Policing*, 2nd ed. (New York: Routledge, 2016), 5.

[7]See *Reducing Crime Through Intelligence-led Policing*, Bureau of Justice Assistance, 2008, https://bja.ojp.gov/sites/g/files/xyckuh186/files/Publications/ReducingCrimeThroughILP.pdf. Jack R. Green notes, "Perhaps like the Old Testament, community and problem-oriented policing begot broken

windows, zero tolerance, hot spots, intelligence-led and now predictive-policing models and their adherents." Jack R. Green, "Zero Tolerance and Policing," in *The Oxford Handbook of Police and Policing*, ed. Michael D. Reisig and Robert J. Kane (New York: Oxford University Press, 2014), 172.

[8]Green summarizes the zero-tolerance approach: "Zero-tolerance policing focuses on police presence and aggressive order maintenance enforcement often for minor misdemeanor behaviors to create a deterrent effect and dissuade those disposed to crime from committing crimes." Green, "Zero Tolerance and Policing," 173.

[9]Green explains, "Zero-tolerance policing seeks to identify and aggressively pursue individuals who violate social convention rather than identifying the underlying causes or conditions giving rise to such behavior." Green, "Zero Tolerance and Policing," 176.

[10]Green writes, "Zero-tolerance policing targets less serious deviance and crime under the idea of 'sending a message' to those in the public square that any and all forms of anti-social behavior will be met with aggressive police action, thereby, deterring such behavior." Green, "Zero Tolerance and Policing," 176.

[11]Green, "Zero Tolerance and Policing," 183.

[12]Green, "Zero Tolerance and Policing," 173.

[13]Green notes, "Zero tolerance comports with the 'crime fighting' image of public policing, but interestingly it negates police discretion and variations in problem-solving: zero tolerance implies the police are compelled to act, no matter the context or circumstances." Green, "Zero Tolerance and Policing," 183.

[14]Alexander argues, "In each generation, new tactics have been used for achieving the same goals—goals shared by the Founding Fathers. Denying African Americans citizenship was deemed essential to the formation of the original union. . . . Rather than rely on race, we use the criminal justice system to label people of color 'criminals' and then engage in all the practices we supposedly left behind." Alexander, *The New Jim Crow*, 1-2.

[15]Alexander, *The New Jim Crow*, 17.

[16]Alexander comments, "Racially biased police discretion is the key to understanding how the overwhelming majority of people who get swept into the criminal justice system in the War on Drugs turn out to be black or brown, even though the police adamantly deny that they engage in racial profiling. In the drug war, police have discretion regarding whom they target (which

individuals), as well as where they target (which neighborhoods or communities)." Alexander, *The New Jim Crow*, 123.

[17]Alexander, *The New Jim Crow*, 124.

[18]Alexander notes, "Tactics that would be political suicide in an upscale white suburb are not even newsworthy in poor black and brown communities. So long as mass drug arrests are concentrated in impoverished urban areas, police chiefs have little reason to fear political backlash, no matter how aggressive and warlike the efforts may be." Alexander, *The New Jim Crow*, 124.

[19]Green, "Zero Tolerance and Policing," 176.

[20]Green, "Zero Tolerance and Policing," 173.

[21]Alexander, *The New Jim Crow,* 17.

[22]Rod K. Brunson and Jacinta M. Gau note, "Blacks in the United States have had a long and tumultuous history of being unjustly targeted, stopped, questioned, and searched by the police. . . . Disproportionate police attention has proven especially harmful to scores of urban black males, who consider themselves officers' primary targets, and who frequently describe their communities as besieged by the police." Rod K. Brunson and Jacinta M. Gau, "Race, Place and Policing the Inner-City," in *The Oxford Handbook of Police and Policing*, ed. Michael D. Reisig and Robert J. Kane (New York: Oxford University Press, 2014), 363.

[23]Rich LeCates, "Intelligence-led Policing: Changing the Face of Crime Prevention," *Police Chief Magazine*, October 17, 2018, www.policechiefmagazine .org/changing-the-face-crime-prevention.

[24]Devon W. Carbado and L. Song Richardson, "The Black Police: Policing Our Own," *Harvard Law Review* 131 (May 2018): 1981.

[25]United States Department of Justice Civil Rights Division and United States Attorney's Office and Western District of Kentucky Civil Division, "Investigation of the Louisville Metro Police Department and Louisville Metro Government," (March 8, 2023), 32, https://www.justice.gov/opa/press-release /file/1573011/download.

[26]US Department of Justice, "Investigation of Louisville Metro PD," 45.

[27]US Department of Justice, "Investigation of Louisville Metro PD," 34.

[28]Ginny Lee, "DOJ Investigation of Lorain Police Department: Case Summary," *Civil Rights Litigation Clearinghouse*, April 6, 2017, https://clearinghouse .net/case/15245.

[29]"How LE Agencies Use Intelligence-Led Policing to Help Cops Catch Criminals and Prevent Attacks," Police 1, January 7, 2016, www.police1.com

/police-products/software/data-information-sharing-software/articles/how
-le-agencies-use-intelligence-led-policing-to-help-cops-catch-criminals-and
-prevent-attacks-xb9hBDdvoKDM2IaY.

[30]United States Department of Justice, "Navigating Your Agency's Path to Intelligence-Led Policing," April 2009, 1, https://bja.ojp.gov/sites/g/files/xyckuh186/files/media/document/navigating_your_agency_s_path_to_intelligence-led_policing.pdf.

[31]This link provides just one example: Bureau of Justice Assistance, U.S. Department of Justice, Funding & Awards, "Intelligence-Led Policing Project," August 23, 2016, https://bja.ojp.gov/funding/awards/2016-dj-bx-0578.

5. SERVANT LEADERSHIP AND FOLLOWERSHIP

[1]Robert K. Greenleaf, *Servant Leadership: A Journey into the Nature of Legitimate Power and Greatness*, anniversary ed. (Mahwah, NJ: Paulist Press, 2002). The first edition was published in 1977. Dirk van Dierendonck and Kathleen Patterson note, "While some would suggest that servant leadership is timeless— or at least as old as time itself, most thinking clusters around the work of Robert Greenleaf, and rightly so." Dirk van Dierendonck and Kathleen Patterson, "Servant Leadership: An Introduction," in *Servant Leadership: Developments in Theory and Research*, ed. Dirk van Dierendonck and Kathleen Patterson (New York: Palgrave Macmillan, 2010), 4. Larry C. Spears states, "The term 'servant leadership' was first coined in a 1970 essay by Robert K. Greenleaf." Larry C. Spears, "Servant Leadership and Robert K. Greenleaf's Legacy," in *Servant Leadership*, ed. van Dierendonck and Patterson, 12.

[2]Greenleaf writes, "Servant and leader—can these two roles be fused in one real person, in all levels of status and calling? If so, can that person live and be productive in the real world of the present? My sense of the present leads me to say yes to both questions." Greenleaf, *Servant Leadership*, 21. Spears explains, "The words 'servant' and 'leader' are usually thought of as being opposites. When two opposites are brought together in a creative and meaningful way, a paradox emerges. And so, the words 'servant' and 'leader' have been brought together to create the paradoxical idea of servant leadership." Spears, "Servant Leadership and Robert K. Greenleaf's Legacy," 12.

[3]Van Dierendonck and Patterson explain, "Within a few short years, our view of what accounts for good leadership has changed dramatically. The ideal of a heroic, hierarchical-oriented leader with primacy to shareholders has quickly been replaced by a view of leadership that gives priority to stewardship, ethical behavior and collaboration through connecting to other

people. . . . As such, it should come as no surprise that interest in servant leadership has risen, and is continuing to rise." Van Dierendonck and Patterson, "Servant Leadership," 3.

[4]Denise L. Parris and John W. Peachy conducted a review of empirical studies of servant leadership and concluded, "There is no consensus on the definition of servant leadership." Denise L. Parris and John W. Peachy, "A Systematic Literature Review of Servant Leadership Theory in Organizational Contexts," *Journal of Business Ethics* 113 (2013): 377.

[5]Sen Sendjaya notes that at a servant leadership conference of scholars, Peter Block said to Larry C. Spears, "You've held on to the spirit of servant leadership, you've kept it vague and undefinable, which I think is a great strategic advantage. People can come every year to figure out what the hell this is." Sen Sendjaya, "Demystifying Servant Leadership," in *Servant Leadership*, ed. van Dierendonck and Patterson, 25. Additionally, Sendjaya notes the problem related to the lack of a definition and "the intentional lack of a formulaic set of rules." Sendjaya, "Demystifying Servant Leadership," 25.

[6]Stephen Prosser, "Opportunities and Tensions of Servant Leadership," in *Servant Leadership*, ed. van Dierendonck and Patterson, 37, emphasis added. Prosser comments, "Servant leadership may well have few established rules and regulations, but the principles lying at the heart are crucial and nonnegotiable: the greatest of these is the commitment to being a servant." Prosser, "Opportunities and Tensions," 37.

[7]Spears, "Servant Leadership and Robert K. Greenleaf's Legacy," 20.

[8]Charles R. Swanson, Leonard Territo, and Robert W. Taylor, "Leadership," in *Police Resources: International Association of Chiefs of Police Promotional Examination Preparation Manual,* edited by the IACP, 1-54. (New York: Pearson, 2012), 40-41.

[9]Peter Northouse explains, "Servant leadership can be applied at all levels of management and in all types of organizations. Within a philosophical framework of caring for others, servant leadership sets forth a list of behaviors that individuals can engage in if they want to be servant leaders. The prescribed behaviors are not esoteric; they are easily understood and generally applicable to a variety of leadership situations." Peter Northouse, *Leadership: Theory and Practice*, 8th ed. (Thousand Oaks, CA: Sage, 2019), 243.

[10]Van Dierendonck and Patterson, "Servant Leadership," 8.

[11]Spears, "Servant Leadership and Robert K. Greenleaf's Legacy," 17-18.

[12]Greenleaf, *Servant Leadership*, 55-56.

[13]Swanson, Territo, and Taylor write, "SLers' emphasis on humility, equality, and empowerment may be seen as weakness." Swanson, Territo, and Taylor, "Leadership," 41.

[14]Swanson, Territo, and Taylor explain, "The theory also fails to take into account how SLers behave when the needs of the organization and the followers are in conflict." Swanson, Territo, and Taylor, "Leadership," 41.

[15]Timothy Robert Cochrell explains, "Greenleaf articulates an extremely optimistic view of human beings and their natural, latent potential to pursue selfless ends, self-actualize, and subsequently meet the needs of individuals within society. He suggests that, given the right social and leadership climate, humanity will, by their own volition, become more caring, ethical, and just. Servant leadership is permeated by humanistic assumptions regarding humanity's ability to create a utopian society through self-actualization and free individual choice." Timothy Robert Cochrell, "Foundations for a Biblical Model of Servant Leadership in the Slave Imagery of Luke–Acts" (PhD diss., The Southern Baptist Theological Seminary, 2015), 7-8.

[16]Cochrell notes that Greenleaf relies on an "eclectic spirituality" and servant leadership is "shaped by a syncretism of Unitarian, Buddhist, and Judeo-Christian principles." Cochrell, "Foundations for a Biblical Model of Servant Leadership," 10.

[17]Friedrich Nietzsche, *Thus Spake Zarathustra* (Hertfordshire: Wordsworth Publishing, 1997), 6.

[18]See Acts 9:6; 2 Corinthians 12; and 1 Corinthians 13.

[19]Nietzsche, *Thus Spake Zarathustra*, 53.

[20]Jeff Myers and David A. Noebel compare worldviews noting the foundational differences in competing worldviews. They illustrate that the worldview shapes beliefs and behaviors, and differing worldviews result in differing beliefs and behaviors: "All people try to make sense of the rules of the world by developing ideas. These ideas flow in patterns, which we call worldviews. People's worldviews lead them to value certain things, which lead to particular convictions governing their behavior. These convictions solidify into habits that affect the way they—and others—live." Jeff Myers and David A. Noebel, *Understanding the Times: A Survey of Competing Worldviews* (Manitou Springs, CO: Summit Ministries, 2015), 7. Furthermore, the authors note that the different worldviews "cannot all depict things as they really are; their competing claims cannot all be true." Myers and Noebel, *Understanding the Times*, 20.

[21]Michael J. Wilder and Timothy Paul Jones, *The God Who Goes Before You: Pastoral Leadership as Christ-Centered Followership* (Nashville: B&H, 2018), 205.

[22]Wilder and Jones, *The God Who Goes Before You*, 3.

[23]Wilder and Jones explain, "The problem is that these principles are presented as if they derive from the biblical metanarrative—and, in particular, from the life and teachings of Jesus—when, in fact, they are the result of human observations of patterns in the created order. The Scriptures are used in ways that are selective, decontextualized, and—in many instances—not even distinctly Christian." Wilder and Jones, *The God Who Goes Before You*, 5.

[24]Wilder and Jones write, "When it comes to leadership, there *is* much to be learned from empirical research and from the intuitive reflections of marketplace leaders—but, without the whole canon of Scripture as our supreme and sufficient authority, flawed views of divine purposes and human capacities will skew our view of leadership. . . . Our goal in this book is to provide a foundation for the study of leadership that looks at the subject with both feet firmly planted in the whole of Scripture, not in a few isolated and extracted examples of leadership." Wilder and Jones, *The God Who Goes Before You*, 8.

[25]Wilder and Jones, *The God Who Goes Before You*, 16.

[26]Wilder and Jones, *The God Who Goes Before You*, 21-24.

[27]Wilder and Jones posit, "The Christian leader is marked by *union* with Christ, *communion* with others, and a *mission* to exercise dominion over some specific aspect of God's creation." Wilder and Jones, *The God Who Goes Before You*, 17.

[28]Wilder and Jones note that union with Christ entails "act[ing] out Christ's obedient sonship." Kevin J. Vanhoozer, "From 'Blessed in Christ' to 'Being in Christ'" in *"In Christ" in Paul*, ed. Michael J. Thate, Kevin J. Vanhoozer, Constantine R. Campbell (Grand Rapids, MI: Eerdmans, 2018), quoted in Wilder and Jones, *The God Who Goes Before You*, 17.

[29]Wilder and Jones suggest, "Union with Christ is identification with God's Son that leads to participation in God's life and to incorporation into the communion of God's people." Wilder and Jones, *The God Who Goes Before You*, 17.

[30]Wilder and Jones explain, "The power that the leader exercises is not the leader's but Christ's, and this power must be expressed according to God's design for a diverse community of Spirit-equipped servants." Wilder and Jones, *The God Who Goes Before You*, 20.

[31]Wilder and Jones note that the Christ-following leader adopts God's mission, which is framed by the "creation mandate" and the "Great Commission." Therefore, the leader has a mission "to exercise dominion over some specific

aspect of God's creation." Wilder and Jones, *The God Who Goes Before You*, 17. Also, Jones and Wilder note that the leader should have a "holy ambition to multiply the manifest fame of God's name and to see people formed into the image of Christ." Wilder and Jones, *The God Who Goes Before You*, 18. Furthermore Jones and Wilder explain, "The truth that the leader is called to proclaim is not the leader's vision but God's revelation." Wilder and Jones, *The God Who Goes Before You*, 20.

[32]Andrew Murray, *Humility and Absolute Surrender* (Peabody, MA: Hendrickson Publishing, 2005), 33.

6. CREATING A NEW VISION FOR POLICE LEADERSHIP

[1]See John David Trentham, "Reading the Social Sciences Theologically (Part 1 & 2): Engaging and Appropriating Models of Human Development," *Christian Educational Journal* 16, no. 3 (2019) for the appropriation concept and protocol. For utilization of the protocol for the servant-shepherd model see Daniel E. Reinhardt, "The Impact of Servant Leadership and Christ-Centered Followership on the Problem of Police Brutality Against Racial Minorities" (PhD diss., The Southern Baptist Theological Seminary, 2021).

[2]Michael J. Wilder and Timothy Paul Jones, *The God Who Goes Before You: Pastoral Leadership as Christ-Centered Followership* (Nashville: B&H, 2018), 21.

[3]Joycelyn M. Pollock writes, "Complete freedom is given up in return for guaranteed protection. Police power is part of this quid pro quo: we give the police these powers in order to protect us." Joycelyn M. Pollock, *Ethical Dilemmas and Decisions in Criminal Justice*, 7th ed. (Belmont, CA: Cengage Learning, 2012), 109. Edwin J. Delattre and Cornelius J. Behan note, "The Founders of the United States believed the public institutions and public servants could aspire to fulfill demanding missions for the public good." Edwin J. Delattre and Cornelius J. Behan, "Practical Ideals for Managing the New Millennium," in *Local Government Police Management*, 4th ed., ed. William A. Geller and Darrel W. Stephens (Wilmette, IL: ICMA Publishers, 2003), 603.

[4]Roger G. Dunham and Geoffrey P. Alpert comment, "Where do the police get the right to use force to control citizens? In a democracy, citizens grant the government (federal, state, and local) the authority to use force to uphold the law. . . . In a democratic state, the people maintain more control over the police. . . . The public surrenders its right to use force and loans that right to the police to use it in the name of the group and to protect each member of the group against the use of force by other members." Roger G. Dunham and Geoffrey P. Alpert, "The Foundation of the Police Role in Society," in *Critical*

Issues in Policing, 7th ed., ed. Roger G. Dunham and Geoffrey P. Alpert (Long Grove, IL: Waveland Press, 2015), 4-5.

[5]Charles R. Swanson, Leonard Territo, and Robert W. Taylor argue for the necessity of clear ethical standards to govern officers. They also provide examples of ethical guidelines and policies that are prevalent in almost all police departments: "The importance of applied ethics is that they help officers develop a reasoned approach to decision making instead of making decisions by habit. As such, a solid ethical background provides a guide for officers making complex moral judgments about depriving people of their liberty and sometimes their lives." Charles R. Swanson, Leonard Territo, and Robert W. Taylor, *Police Administration: Structures, Processes, and Behaviors*, 8th ed. (Upper Saddle River, NJ: Pearson, 2012), 122.

[6]Pollock notes, "The law governs many of the decisions that public servants make, but because of the discretion that exists . . . all professionals in the criminal justice field must be sensitive to ethical issues." Pollock, *Ethical Dilemmas and Decisions*, 6.

[7]Pollock explains that the police "are public servants. Their salaries come from the public purse. Public servants possess more than a job; they have taken on special duties involving the public trust. . . . Arguably, they must be held to higher standards than those they guard or govern." Pollock, *Ethical Dilemmas and Decisions*, 6.

[8]Delattre and Behan, "Practical Ideals," 603.

[9]Christians would recognize that the authority that rests in the government has been ultimately placed there by God (Romans 13:1). Thus, submission to governing authorities is submission to God. This association, however, is not completely necessary. The non-Christian leader must simply recognize that power has been delegated to them by a higher authority, namely, the government of the people, and they are to submit to that authority and follow first.

[10]The term *church* is not used to reference a building or a place of worship. *Church* in this context references the people of the church. In other words, the term *church* means the collective of Christians.

[11]Wilder and Jones explain, "The position to which the leader is called is not sovereignty above or separation from the community but stewardship within the community in union with Christ." Wilder and Jones, *The God Who Goes Before You*, 20.

[12]Wilder and Jones write, "In God's eyes, all of humankind is royalty. Every child of Adam and Eve from every ethnicity and culture is, therefore, equally

and infinitely valuable. As a result, the people we lead must be defined in our minds first and foremost 'by their creation in the image of God. . . . They are not problems to be fixed, but mysteries to be honored and revered.'" Wilder and Jones, *The God Who Goes Before You*, 30.

[13]Wilder and Jones explain, "This shared status of sonship and rulership did not, however, preclude the possibility of hierarchies, ranks, or distinct responsibilities among the first human beings." Wilder and Jones, *The God Who Goes Before You*, 30.

[14]Wilder and Jones note that the leader "develops a diverse community of fellow laborers who are equipped and empowered to pursue shared goals." Wilder and Jones, *The God Who Goes Before You*, 20.

[15]Wilder and Jones posit, "Authority is divinely delegated to us for a purpose greater than ourselves. Power and authority belong to God, not to us." Wilder and Jones, *The God Who Goes Before You*, 20. Dunham and Alpert, "The Foundation of the Police Role in Society," 4-5.

[16]Wilder and Jones assert, "Authority is never our own property to be used as we please." Wilder and Jones, *The God Who Goes Before You*, 20.

[17]Wilder and Jones, *The God Who Goes Before You*, 20.

[18]Wilder and Jones explain, "The creation mandate is God's command to humanity to 'be fruitful, multiply, fill the earth, and subdue it' (Genesis 1:28). 'Be fruitful, multiply, fill the earth' suggest cultivation of the social world. . . . 'Subdue the earth' includes stewardship of the natural world." Wilder and Jones, *The God Who Goes Before You*, 17.

[19]Wilder and Jones note that because of original sin, the present world is systemically problematic: "But humanity refused to be satisfied with anything less than total sovereignty. The resulting rebellion birthed not only personal iniquity but also the spread of sin in social structures, resulting in systemic injustice and oppression." Wilder and Jones, *The God Who Goes Before You*, 32.

[20]Wilder and Jones tie mission to the creation mandate and the Great Commission and note that mission involves exercising "dominion over some aspect of God's creation." Wilder and Jones, *The God Who Goes Before You*, 17.

[21]Sir Robert Peel, quoted in George L. Kelling, "The Evolution of Contemporary Policing," in *Local Government Police Management,* 4th ed., ed. William A. Geller and Darrel W. Stephens (Wilmette, IL: ICMA Publishers, 2003), 3.

[22]Sir Robert Peel, quoted in Pamela D. Mayhall, *Police-Community Relations and the Administration of Justice* (New York: John Wiley and Sons, 1985), 20.

[23]M. A. Lewis notes that Peel's reforms and principles were a reaction by evangelical Christians to the injustice of the legal system: "British evangelicals long had protested Britain's legal and penal system; its law enforcement strategy involved tactics that some citizens found intimidating. . . . Peel was sympathetic to these evangelicals." M. A. Lewis, "Peel's Legacy," *The FBI Law Enforcement Bulletin* 80, no. 12 (December 2011): 8.

[24]Wilder and Jones, *The God Who Goes Before You*, 110.

[25]Wilder and Jones, *The God Who Goes Before You*, 117.

[26]When Jesus "saw the crowds, he had compassion for them, because they were harassed and helpless, like sheep without a shepherd" (Matthew 9:36).

[27]Wilder and Jones, *The God Who Goes Before You*, 125.

[28]Wilder and Jones, *The God Who Goes Before You*, 175.

[29]Wilder explains, "I readily acknowledge that I am simply a brother among a family, a brother who has been asked to lead." Wilder and Jones, *The God Who Goes Before You*, 176. The concept of brotherhood is not foreign to police officers. Jerome H. Skolnick and James J. Fyfe note that the police share a culture, face danger, and exercise authority: "This combination generates and supports norms of internal solidarity, or *brotherhood*." Emphasis original. Jerome H. Skolnick and James J. Fyfe, *Above the Law: Police and the Excessive Use of Force* (New York: Free Press, 1993), 92. I have been part of the Fraternal Order of Police (FOP)—the largest police union in the United States—for over twenty years. After one year of service, officers join the FOP and the occasion is marked by a celebration that follows the swearing-in ceremony. At FOP functions, officers refer to each other as brother. It has been my experience that the brotherhood dynamic is embedded in the police culture.

[30]Wilder notes that Peter emphasized this relationship: "It seems to be a deliberate mind-set and intentional approach to ministry for Peter, as he avoids using language that would elevate himself." Wilder and Jones, *The God Who Goes Before You*, 176.

[31]Christians understand themselves as delivered from the old life or way of living and look forward to the final consummation of God's kingdom. However, the journey—or the current time—is part of the sojourn to the end. Thus, Christians identify as ultimately redeemed yet realize they are on an imperfect journey until God's kingdom is consummated. Wilder notes, "Peter wants these people to be convinced when they look in the mirror that they are looking at a redeemed person upon whom God has lavished his love

and mercy. But he knows that is not enough. He wants to balance that eternal truth with the momentary reality that Christians still have a life to live between now and then. It is not enough for them to see themselves as the redeemed; they must also see themselves as *redeemed sojourners*." Wilder and Jones, *The God Who Goes Before You*, 186.

[32]Wilder explains, "Peter continues to inform his flock's identity by telling them, 'You yourselves like living stones are being built up as a spiritual house, to be a holy priesthood' (1 Peter 2:5 ESV). Coming on the heels of celebrating their redemption, these words emphasize that these believers had been made part of the most amazing and glorious house ever constructed. . . . The language that is used in 1 Peter 2:4-10 points toward the Jewish temple and the role of the priests there. In the Old Testament, the temple was the place where God promised to meet with his people. Together, the priests and the people were responsible for representing God and his rule to the world." Wilder and Jones, *The God Who Goes Before You*, 187.

[33]Wilder notes that pastors can try to hide the reality that Christians suffer and notes how Peter wrote concerning suffering: "Peter, who identifies himself as a witness of the sufferings of Christ, does just the opposite. He does not sugarcoat the Christian experience. He makes it clear that the Christian journey is marked by suffering and that Jesus himself is the model for how his followers are to endure such suffering." Wilder and Jones, *The God Who Goes Before You*, 188.

[34]Steven G. Brandl and Meagan S. Stoshine comment, "Even though injuries that result from assaults are relatively rare in police work . . . the likely psychological effects of injuries that result from these interactions may likely have dramatic long-term negative consequences for officers' physical and emotional well-being and as such may be much more significant than injuries in other ways." Steven G. Brandl and Meagan S. Stoshine, "Toward an Understanding of the Physical Hazards of Police Work," in *Critical Issues in Policing*, 398.

[35]Jones notes that pastors must be accessible and willing to "spend time with the flock" to "understand how [they] view the world." Wilder and Jones, *The God Who Goes Before You*, 124-125.

[36]Larry C. Spears, "Servant Leadership and Robert K. Greenleaf's Legacy," in *Servant Leadership: Developments in Theory and Research*, ed. Dirk van Dierendonck and Kathleen Patterson (New York: Palgrave Macmillan, 2010), 17.

[37]Spears, "Servant Leadership and Robert K. Greenleaf's Legacy," 17.

[38]Spears explains, "General awareness, and especially self-awareness, strengthens the servant-leader. . . . 'Awareness is not a giver of solace—it is just the opposite. It is a disturber and an awakener.'" Spears, "Servant Leadership and Robert K. Greenleaf's Legacy," 17-18.

[39]Spears, "Servant Leadership and Robert K. Greenleaf's Legacy," 19.

7. FINDING TRUE NORTH

[1]John Stott, *The Message of Romans* (Downers Grove, IL: IVP Academic, 1994), 323-324.

[2]James H. Cone profoundly captures the pain and anguish of a history of atrocities: "For African Americans the memory of disfigured black bodies 'swinging in the southern breeze' is so painful that they, too, try to keep these horrors buried deep down in their consciousness, until, like a dormant volcano, they erupt uncontrollably, causing profound agony and pain. But as with the evils of chattel slavery and Jim Crow segregation, blacks and whites and other Americans who want to understand the true meaning of the American experience need to remember lynching. To forget the atrocity leaves us with a fraudulent perspective of this society." James H. Cone, *The Cross and the Lynching Tree* (Maryknoll, NY: Orbis Books, 2018), xiv.

[3]Oxiris Barbot reflects, "When I think of the torture and murder of George Floyd at the knee of a White police officer, I feel morally wounded. We've been here before, with countless Black men and woman whose lives were taken by those who wielded unearned power over them." Oxiris Barbot, "George Floyd and Our Collective Moral Injury," *American Journal of Public Health* 110, no. 9 (2020): 1253.

[4]Stanley J. Grenz, *The Moral Quest: Foundations of Christian Ethics* (Downers Grove, IL: IVP Academic, 1997), 114.

[5]J. P. Moreland and William Craig, *Philosophical Foundations for a Christian Worldview* (Downers Grove, IL: IVP Academic, 2003), 446.

[6]Malcolm D. Holmes and Brad W. Smith explain, "Blacks see the police as oppressors protecting the interests of the white community. . . . Many minority citizens perceive the police as a real danger in their day-to-day lives." Malcolm D. Homes and Brad W. Smith, *Race and Police Brutality: Roots of an Urban Dilemma* (Albany: State University of New York Press, 2008), 2-6. The authors note that racial minorities perceive the police as a legitimate threat to their safety. Furthermore, the police are often understood as oppressors rather than public servants who are interested in helping the community. Holmes and Smith, *Race and Police Brutality*, 2-6. Gina Robertiello confirms,

"Surveys consistently show Blacks are less likely than Whites to trust local police and to treat both races equally." Gina Robertiello, *The Use and Abuse of Police Power in America* (Santa Barbara, CA: ABC-CLIO, 2017), 213.

[7]Moreland and Craig assert, "[Kant] is still regarded as the most important advocate of the position." Moreland and Craig, *Philosophical Foundations*, 449.

[8]For a comprehensive treatment of Kant's ethic as it relates to law enforcement see Daniel E. Reinhardt, "The Impact of Servant Leadership and Christ-Centered Followership on the Problem of Police Brutality Against Racial Minorities," (PhD diss., The Southern Baptist Theological Seminary, 2021).

[9]Grenz provides a basic understanding of the categorical imperative. Grenz, *The Moral Quest*, 32.

[10]Sir Robert Peel, quoted in George L. Kelling, "The Evolution of Contemporary Policing," *Local Government Police Management*, 4th ed., ed. William A. Geller and Darrel W. Stephens (Wilmette, IL: ICMA Publishers, 2003), 3.

[11]Grenz, *The Moral Quest*, 114.

[12]Wayne Grudem, *Systematic Theology: An Introduction to Biblical Doctrine* (Grand Rapids, MI: Zondervan, 2000), 450.

[13]Grudem, *Systematic Theology*, 450.

[14]R. E. O. White, "Reconciliation," in *The Evangelical Dictionary of Theology*, 2nd ed., ed. Walter A. Elwell (Grand Rapids, MI: Baker Academic, 2001), 992.

[15]Andreas J. Kostenberger, *Biblical Theology for Christian Proclamation: Commentary on 1-2 Timothy and Titus* (Nashville: B&H, 2017), 193.

[16]W. E. Vine, *Vine's Expository Dictionary of Old and New Testament Words* (Nashville: Thomas Nelson, 1997), 728.

[17]It should be noted the paragraphs that described modifying Kant's ethic directly reflects John David Trentham's protocol of inverse consistency explained earlier.

8. TRANSFORMATION THROUGH LEADERSHIP

[1]W. Warner Burke explains, "Revolutionary change . . . can be seen as a jolt (perturbation) to the system." W. Warner Burke, *Organizational Change: Theory and Practice*, 5th ed. (Thousand Oaks, CA: Sage, 2018), 77. He also explains, "Deep Structure . . . is perhaps the key concept for understanding the nature of revolutionary change." Burke, *Organizational Change*, 99.

[2]Burke defines deep structure as "the underlying culture, the structure itself—that is, organizational design for decision making, accountability, control, and distribution of power—and the way the organization monitors,

reacts to, and in general, relates to its external environment." Burke, *Organizational Change*, 76.

[3]Burke posits, "Organizations that change their missions exemplify revolutionary change." Burke, *Organizational Change*, 77.

[4]Edgar H. Schein, *Organizational Culture and Leadership*, 5th ed. (Hoboken, NJ: John Wiley and Sons, 2017), 18.

[5]Schein notes through the use of a metaphor that the first two levels will not result in true cultural change and concludes that to change culture, leaders "have to locate the cultural DNA and change some of that." Schein, *Organizational Culture and Leadership*, 25-26.

[6]Burke notes regarding cultural change: "The focus was on behavior that was intended to counter the basic assumptions." Burke, *Organizational Change*, 257.

[7]James M. Kouzes and Barry Z. Posner, *The Leadership Challenge*, 6th ed. (Hoboken, NJ: John Wiley and Sons, 2017), 20.

[8]Kouzes and Posner, *The Leadership Challenge*, 12-13.

[9]Charles R. Swanson, Leonard Territo, and Robert W. Taylor, *Police Administration: Structures, Processes, and Behaviors*, 8th ed. (Upper Saddle River, NJ: Pearson, 2012), 286.

[10]Kouzes and Posner, *The Leadership Challenge*, 12.

[11]Kouzes and Posner, *The Leadership Challenge*, 12-13.

[12]Kouzes and Posner, *The Leadership Challenge*, 13.

[13]Kouzes and Posner, *The Leadership Challenge*, 13.

[14]Kouzes and Posner write, "Leaders *recognize contributions by showing appreciation for individual excellence. . . .* Being a leader requires showing appreciation for people's contributions and creating a culture of *celebrating the values and victories by creating a spirit of community*." Kouzes and Posner, *The Leadership Challenge*, 19, emphasis original.

9. A NEW STRATEGY OF PEACE

[1]This was the common terminology used at the time for arrests.

[2]Unfortunately, like many police departments at the time, we thought community policing was a unit and not a philosophy. That is why there was such disparity between the philosophy and methodology of the small community policing unit and the overall department. Also, like many urban police departments at the time, we were facing financial problems. Therefore, I was placed in a community policing unit without ever being sent to community policing training.

[3]Radley Balko, *Rise of the Warrior Cop: The Militarization of America's Police Forces* (New York: Public Affairs, 2013), 325-26.

[4]Balko, *Rise of the Warrior Cop*, 326-32.

[5]Gary W. Cordner, "Community Policing," in *The Oxford Handbook of Police and Policing*, ed. Michael D. Reisig and Robert J. Kane (New York: Oxford University Press, 2014), 159.

[6]Rod K. Brunson and Jacinta M. Gau, "Race, Place and Policing the Inner-City," in *The Oxford Handbook of Police and Policing*, 367.

[7]Brunson and Gau note, "The outcomes of police legitimacy are generally conceived of as compliance with the criminal law and cooperation with the police." Brunson and Gau, "Race, Place and Policing the Inner-City," 368.

[8]Brunson and Gau, "Race, Place and Policing the Inner-City," 365.

[9]Brunson and Gau, "Race, Place and Policing the Inner-City," 367.

[10]Cordner explains, "Community policing recommends re-oriented operations, with less reliance on the patrol car and more emphasis on face-to-face interactions. . . . Community policing tries to implement a prevention emphasis. . . . Community policing adopts a geographic focus to establish stronger bonds between officers and neighborhoods." Cordner, "Community Policing," 155-56.

[11]Cordner notes that enforcement is an inevitable practice of law enforcement. Thus, "community policing recognizes this fact and recommends that officers offset it as much as they can by engaging in positive interactions whenever possible." Cordner, "Community Policing," 156.

[12]Cordner posits, "Community policing stresses active partnerships . . . in which all parties really work together to identify and solve problems." In doing so, the author notes that "officers should search for underlying conditions." Cordner, "Community Policing," 156.

[13]Michael J. Wilder and Timothy Paul Jones write, "The Christ-following leader—living as a bearer of God's image in union with Christ and his people—develops a diverse community of fellow laborers who are equipped and empowered to pursue shared goals that fulfill the creation mandate and the Great Commission in submission to the Word of God." Michael J. Wilder and Timothy Paul Jones, *The God Who Goes Before You: Pastoral Leadership as Christ-Centered Followership* (Nashville: B&H, 2018), 16. Wilder and Jones ground the value of humanity in the Christian concept of the image of God in all people. However, the officer must simply affirm the equal value of every ethnicity and race.

[14]John M. Perkins writes, quoting Dave Unander: "Dave warns the church about the 'myth of race' and the ways that we've allowed cultural understandings of race to infect our theology and how we view each other. 'There is only one race,' he writes, 'from every perspective: biological, historical, and in God's Word, the Bible. For the past five hundred years, Western society has been playing out a role in a drama written by the Enemy of our souls, the myth of the master race, and every act has been a tragedy. It's time to change the script.'" John M. Perkins, *One Blood: Parting Words to the Church on Race and Love* (Chicago: Moody Press, 2018), 47.

[15]Wilder and Jones, *The God Who Goes Before You*, 110.

[16]Wilder and Jones, *The God Who Goes Before You*, 117.

[17]Jones provides a helpful guideline for pastors that is applicable to enforcement from a protection perspective: "Godly leadership is followership exercised with biblical wisdom for the good and guidance of a community for which God has given us responsibility. Any power we possess has been divinely delegated to guide God's flock toward his purposes and his peace." Wilder and Jones, *The God Who Goes Before You*, 122.

[18]See Matthew 9:36.

[19]In response to the problem of single-parent households and the absence of fathers, Eric Mason asserts, "Shepherds in the church function as spiritual fathers to those who lack a godly image of a man in the home and world." Eric Mason, quoted in Wilder and Jones, *The God Who Goes Before You*, 126.

10. IMPACTING A HURTING DEMOGRAPHIC

[1]By *investment*, I mean how police practices have affected the community, particularly the relationship with the community. In a sense, all police actions are an investment in a future outcome relationally with the communities they serve. Essentially, the police by and large invested in tactics and crime-fighting strategies that alienated and angered many people.

[2]Crack pipes are usually improvised instruments such as a small glass tube or a hollow antenna piece. Usually, it was much easier to catch a crack user than a crack dealer. The users were generally far more careless and in perpetual possession of a crack pipe.

[3]Although union with Christ is fundamental to the Christian identity, the term *identity* in this chapter is used as typically understood and applied in the social sciences. Harry W. Gardiner notes, "Psychologist Erik Erikson is generally credited with the first complete analysis of identity development," and explains, "Identity is a person's self-definition as a separate and distinct

individual, including behaviors, beliefs, and attitudes." Harry W. Gardiner, *Lives Across Cultures: Cross-Cultural Human Development* (New York: Pearson, 2018), 89.

[4]See James H. Cone, *The Cross and the Lynching Tree* (Maryknoll, NY: Orbis Books, 2018), xiv.

[5]Gina Robertiello explains the role of the police historically starting from the 1600s to the current era. In doing so, she notes key events such as an early form of law enforcement utilized to return escaped slaves to their owners, law enforcement during the civil rights movement, and current events that have led to civil unrest and tension between the police and racial minorities. Gina Robertiello, *The Use and Abuse of Police Power in America* (Santa Barbara, CA: ABC-CLIO, 2017).

[6]Malcolm D. Holmes and Brad W. Smith, *Race and Police Brutality: Roots of an Urban Dilemma* (Albany: State University of New York Press, 2008), 5.

[7]For an in-depth analysis of police culture see Holmes and Smith. They explain that police officers have a formative subculture that results in a social identity. The social identity of police officers is disparate from the social identity of racial minorities. This disparity contributes to social distance and ultimately leads to a proclivity for abuse. Holmes and Smith, *Race and Police Brutality*.

[8]Peter Molenaar, Richard M. Lerner, and Karl M. Newell, "Developmental Systems Theory and Methodology: A View of the Issues," in *The Handbook of Developmental Systems Theory and Methodology*, ed. Peter Molenaar, Richard M. Lerner, and Karl M. Newell (New York: Guilford, 2013), 3.

[9]Aerika S. Brittian, "Understanding African American Adolescents' Identity Development: A Relational Developmental Systems Perspective," *Journal of Black Psychology* 38, no. 2 (2012): 172-200.

[10]Molenaar, Lerner, and Newell write, "There exists a long tradition in theoretical psychology and theoretical biology in which developmental processes are explained as the result of self-organizing processes with emergent properties that have complex, dynamic interactions with environmental influences." Molenaar, Lerner, and Newell, "Developmental Systems Theory and Methodology," 3.

[11]Richard M. Lerner et al., "Using Relational Developmental Systems Theory to Link Program Goals, Activities, and Outcomes: The Sample of the 4-H Study of Positive Youth Development," *New Direction for Youth Development* 144 (Winter 2014): 18.

[12]Gardiner, *Lives across Cultures*, 89.

[13]Commenting on the period of adolescence, Gardiner notes, "The individual is trying to answer the question, 'Who am I?' Finding the answer isn't always easy and involves many of those within one's various ecological systems, including family and friends, members of peer groups, and teachers." Gardiner, *Lives Across Cultures*, 89. Deborah Rivas-Drake et al. note, "[Ethnic and racial identity] in adolescence supports the notion that it is a period of increased meaning-making around the complexities of ethnic and racial group membership." Deborah Rivas-Drake et al., "Ethnic and Racial Identity in Adolescence: Implications for Psychosocial, Academic, and Health Outcomes," *Child Development* 85, no. 1 (January/February 2014): 41.

[14]Robert S. Feldman reviews Erickson's and Marcia's theories of identity formation, noting the similarities and contrasts. Nonetheless, he concludes that "adolescence often brings substantial changes in teenagers' self-concepts and self-esteem—in sum, their notions of their own identity." Robert S. Feldman, *Development across the Life Span*, 5th ed. (Upper Saddle River, NJ: Pearson, 2008), 409-14.

[15]Rivas-Drake et al. note, "Identities linked to ethnicity or race can be developed based on cultural background (e.g., values, traditions) or specific experiences (e.g., racial discrimination) resulting from self-perceived ethnic or racial group membership." Rivas-Drake et al., "Ethnic and Racial Identity," 41.

[16]William E. Cross and T. Binta Cross, "Theory, Research and Models," in *The Handbook of Race, Racism, and the Developing Child*, edited by Stephen M. Quintana and Clark McKown (Hoboken, NJ: John Wiley and Sons, 2008), 171.

[17]Cross and Cross, "Theory, Research and Models," 172.

[18]Robert M. Sellers, Mia A. Smith, J. Nicole Shelton, Stephanie A. J. Rowley, and Tabbye M. Chavous, "Multidimensional Model of Racial Identity: A Reconceptualization of African American Racial Identity," *Personality and Social Psychology Review* 2, no. 1 (1998): 24-27.

[19]Sellers et al., "Multidimensional Model of Racial Identity," 29.

[20]Victor E. Kappeler, Richard D. Sluder, and Geoffrey P. Alpert, "Breeding Deviant Conformity: The Ideology and Culture of Police," in *Critical Issues in Policing*, 7th ed., ed. Roger G. Dunham and Geoffrey P. Alpert (Long Grove, IL: Waveland Press, 2015), 84.

[21]Kappeler, Sluder, and Alpert note the hiring practices in law enforcement have led to a disproportionate number of middle-class White male officers that "are unable to identify with groups on the margins of traditional society." Kappeler, Sluder, and Alpert, "Breeding Deviant Conformity," 84.

²²See Holmes and Smith, *Race and Police Brutality*, 93. See also Jeff Pegues, *Black and Blue: Inside the Divide between the Police and Black America* (Amherst, NY: Prometheus Books, 2017), 120.

²³Robertiello, *The Use and Abuse of Police Power*, 213.

²⁴Holmes and Smith write, "The contrast between the police and minorities is stark, prompting the activation of social identity processes that will create ingroup cohesion and ethnocentrism in situations where they face one another." Holmes and Smith, *Race and Police Brutality*, 53. They continue, "Certainly, those conditions exacerbate police-minority tensions and set the stage for police brutality." Holmes and Smith, *Race and Police Brutality*, 55.

²⁵Tiffany Nicole Lockett writes, "Racism and discrimination impact how the dominant culture labels African American males as the *symbolic assailants* or 'everyday criminal' while at the same time influencing how African American men view themselves." Tiffany Nicole Lockett, "Effects of Racism and Discrimination on Personality Development among African American Male Repeat Offenders" (MA diss., California State Polytechnic University, 2013), 51.

²⁶Callie Harbin Burt, Ronald L. Simmons, and Frederick X. Gibbons note, "We specify a social psychological model linking personal experiences with racial discrimination to an increased risk of offending. . . . We find that racial discrimination is positively associated with increased crime in large part by augmenting depression, hostile views of relationships, and disengagement from conventional norms." Callie Harbin Burt, Ronald L. Simmons, and Frederick X. Gibbons, "Racial Discrimination, Ethnic Racial Socialization, and Crime: A Micro-Sociological Model of Risk and Resilience," *American Sociological Review* 77, no. 4 (2012): 648.

²⁷Derrick P. Jones concludes, "Themes that were identified from the data collected and analyzed revealed that the perceptions of the police contributed to African Americans [*sic*] resentment of the police, which frequently results in violence and loss of human life." Derrick P. Jones, "The Police Strategy of Racial Profiling and Its Impact on African Americans" (PhD diss., Walden University, 2014), 4.

²⁸Rod K. Brunson and Jody Miller note the "disproportionate effects of police practices and misconduct on African Americans in the United States" and "specifically minorities that are young and male bear the largest share of the negative experiences." Rod K. Brunson and Jody Miller, "Young Black Men and Urban Policing in the United States," *The British Journal of Criminology* 46 (2006): 614.

[29]Brunson references existing research and concludes, "Blacks not only draw from their own experiences, but also follow patterns of events they are exposed to in their communities and knowledge imparted by members of their racial group." Rod K. Brunson, "Police Don't Like Black People: African-American Accumulated Police Experiences, *Criminology and Public Policy* 6, no. 1 (2007): 72.